The Release

of the

SPIRIT

...

Watchman Nee

...

Published

for

SURE FOUNDATION

CONTENTS

Introduction

Preface

IN READING this manuscript we have been impressed that it is a vital message needing to be shared and known by all the Lord's seeking ones who long to be a channel for His Life. One cannot read very far before sensing Watchman Nee's longing and prayer is that the Church may know the Lord in the fullest way, that God's people may be increasingly fruitful unto Him, that He may find a minimum of hindrance in us, and that He may be fully released through our quickened and controlled spirit.

Surely this is the hour when the battleground is in the soul. While the Lord is seeking to work through the quickened spirit, Satan is seeking to work through the natural, soulish life which has not been brought under control of the Spirit.

In his many years of laboring with fellow workers, Brother Nee has clearly seen the absolute necessity of brokenness. It is almost as if he were personally here upon the religious scene in America sensing the great need for brokenness among Christian workers. There may be some who are unprepared for such a bitter dose of spiritual medicine, yet we believe anyone with discernment and hunger will agree that the breaking of the soul-powers is imperative if the human spirit is to express the Life of the Lord Jesus.

Second Preface — October 1976

Rejoice with us! One million copies in ten languages are now in print. In this present hour, when the religious scene is occupied with subjectivism and emotional experiences, it seems even more important (than it was twelve years ago when this book was first published) that each one of God's children understand his basic make-up and function of his spirit, soul and body. For those who are truly pressing for the prize and the upward calling this is indeed a truth most imperative. We trust then that this message shall reach every part of the Body of Christ and accomplish a release of His life. May it be so for His eternal glory, praise and honor!

The Publishers

Introduction

FOR THE READER to properly appreciate these lessons, perhaps a few preparatory statements will be helpful:

Firstly, we must become accustomed to the terminology which Brother Nee uses. He has chosen to call man's spirit the inner man; he calls man's soul the outer man and for the body he uses the term, the outermost man. In the diagram we have pictured this. It will also help to realize that in designing man originally, God intended for man's spirit to be His home or dwelling place. So the Holy Spirit making a union with the human spirit was to govern the soul, and the spirit and soul would use the body as the means of expression.

Secondly, when Watchman Nee speaks of destroying the soul, it may seem he is using too strong a word as though to imply annihilation. Actually the whole substance of his mes-

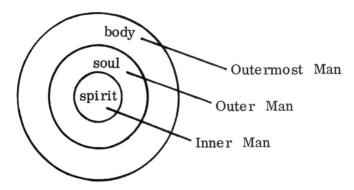

sage clearly points out that the soul, instead of functioning independently, must become the organ or vessel for the spirit. So it is the independent action of the soul that must be destroyed. T. Austin-Sparks has wisely pointed out:

> "We must be careful that, in recognizing the fact that the soul has been seduced, led captive, darkened and poisoned with a self-interest, we do not regard it as something to be annihilated and destroyed in this life. This would be asceticism, a form of Buddhism. The result of any such behavior is usually only another form of soulishness in an exaggerated degree; perhaps occultism. Our whole human nature is in our souls, and if nature is suppressed in one direction she will take revenge in another. This is just what is the trouble with a great many people if only they knew it. There is a difference between a life of suppression and a life of service. Submission, subjection and servanthood in Christ's case, as to the Father, was not a life of soul-destruction, but of rest and delight. Slavery in its bad sense is the lot of those who live wholly in their own souls. We need to revise our ideas about service, for it is becoming more and more common to think that service is bondage and slavery; when really it is a Divine thing. Spirituality is not a life of suppression. That is negative. Spirituality is positive; it is a new and extra life, not the old one striving to get the mastery of itself."

Thirdly, we must see how the soul has to be smitten a fatal blow by the death of Christ as to its self-strength and government. As with Jacob's thigh, after God had touched it he went to the end of his life with a limp. This would illustrate clearly that forever there must be registered in the soul the fact that it cannot and must not act out from itself as the source. Again T. Austin-Sparks writes: "As an instrument the soul has to be won, mastered and ruled in relation to the higher and different ways of God. It is spoken of so frequently in the Scriptures as being some thing over which we have to gain and exercise authority. For instance:

'In your patience ye shall win your
    souls.'   Luke 21:19
'Ye have purified your souls in your

obedience to the truth.'   I Pet. 1:22
'The end of your faith, even the
salvation of your souls.'   I Pet. 1:9."

Finally, in these lessons we must see why Watchman Nee insists that the soul (outer man) be broken, be mastered and be renewed for the spirit to use. T. Austin-Sparks has said:

"Whether we are able yet to accept it or not, the fact is that if we are going on with God fully, all the soul's energies and abilities for knowing, understanding, sensing and doing will come to an end, and we shall—on that side—stand bewildered, dazed, numbed and impotent. Then, only a new, other, and Divine understanding, constraint, and energy will send us forward or keep us going. At such times we shall have to say to our souls, 'My soul, be thou silent unto God' (Ps. 62.5); and 'My soul, come thou with me to follow the Lord.' But what joy and strength there is when, the soul having been constrained to yield to the spirit, the higher wisdom and glory is perceived in its vindication. Then it is that 'My soul doth magnify the Lord, and my spirit hath rejoiced in God my Saviour" (Luke 1:46). The spirit HATH, the soul DOTH—note the tenses.

So that unto fullness of joy the soul is essential, and it MUST be brought through the darkness and death of its own ability to learn the higher and deeper realities for which the spirit is the first organ and faculty."*

As we approach the end of these lessons we shall have found the secret of fruitful living unto HIM. Do not fall into the snare, as so many have, of trying to suppress your soul or of despising it; but be strong in spirit, so that your soul may be won, saved and made to serve His fullest joy. The Lord Jesus has planned that we should find rest unto our souls, and this, He says, comes by way of His yoke—the symbol of union and service. We shall then appreciate how the soul finds its greatest value in service, not in ruling. True, until broken, the soul wants to be master. Through the Cross it can become a very useful servant.

*(Quotes from: WHAT IS MAN by T. Austin-Sparks)

The Importance

of Brokenness

ANYONE who serves God will discover sooner or later that the great hindrance to his work is not others but himself. He will discover that his outward man and his inward man are not in harmony, for both are tending toward opposite directions. He will also sense the inability of his outward man to submit to the spirit's control, thus rendering him incapable of obeying God's highest commands. He will quickly detect that the greatest difficulty lies in his outward man, for it hinders him from using his spirit.

Many of God's servants are not able to do even the most elementary works. Ordinarily they should be enabled by the exercise of their spirit to know God's word, to discern the spiritual condition of another, to send forth God's messages under anointing and to receive God's revelations. Yet due to the distractions of the outward man, their spirit does not seem to function properly. It is basically because their outward man has never been dealt with. For this reason revival, zeal, pleading and activity are but a waste of time. As we shall see, there is just one basic dealing which can enable man to be useful before God: brokenness.

The Inward Man and the Outward Man

Notice how the Bible divides man into two parts: "For I delight in the law of God according to the inward man" (Rom. 7:22). Our inward man delights in the Law of God. ". . . To be strengthened with power by his Spirit in the inner man" (Eph. 3:16). And Paul also tells us, "But if indeed our outward man is consumed, yet the inward is renewed day by day" (2 Cor. 4:16).

When God comes to indwell us by His Spirit, life and power, He comes into our spirit which we are calling the inward man. Outside of this inward man is the soul wherein function our thoughts, emotions and will. The outermost man is our physical body. Thus we will speak of the inward man as the spirit, the outer man as the soul and the outermost man as the body. We must never forget that our inward man is the human spirit where God dwells, where His Spirit mingles with our spirit. Just as we are dressed in clothes, so our inward man "wears" an outward man: the spirit "wears" the soul. And similarly, the spirit and soul "wear" the body. It is quite evident that men are generally more conscious of the outer and outermost man, and they hardly recognize or understand their spirit at all.

We must know that he who can work for God is the one whose inward man can be released. The basic difficulty of a servant of God lies in the failure of the inward man to break through the outward man. Therefore we must recognize before God that the first difficulty to our work is not in others but in ourselves. Our spirit seems to be wrapped in a covering so that it cannot easily break forth. If we have never learned how to release our inward man by breaking through the outward man, we are not able to serve. Nothing can so hinder us as this outward man. Whether our works are fruitful or not depends upon whether our outward man has been broken by the Lord so that the inward man can pass through that brokenness and come forth. This is the basic problem. The Lord wants to break our outward man in order that the inward man may have a way out. When the inward man is released, both unbelievers and Christians will be blessed.

Nature Has Its Way of Breaking

The Lord Jesus tells us in John 12, "Except the grain of wheat falling into the ground die, it abides alone; but if it die, it bears much fruit." Life is in the grain of wheat, but there is a shell, a very hard shell on the outside. As long as that shell is not split open, the wheat cannot sprout and grow. "Except the grain of wheat falling into the ground die . . . " What is this death? It is the cracking open of the shell through the working together of temperature, humidity, in the soil. Once the shell is split open, the wheat begins to grow. So the question here is not whether there is life within, but whether the outside shell is cracked open.

The Scripture continues by saying, "He that loves his life (Greek, *soul*) shall lose it, and he that hates his life (Greek, *soul*) in this world shall keep it to life eternal" (v. 25). The Lord shows us here that the outer shell is our own life (our soul life), while the life within is the eternal life which He has given to us. To allow the inner life to come forth, it is imperative that the outward life be replaced. Should the outward remain unbroken, the inward would never be able to come forth.

It is necessary (in this writing) that we direct these words to that group of people who have the Lord's life. Among those who possess the life of the Lord can be found two distinct conditions: one includes those in whom life is confined, restricted, imprisoned and unable to come forth; the other includes those in whom the Lord has forged a way, and life is thus released from them.

The question thus is not how to obtain life, but rather how

to allow this life to come forth. When we say we need the Lord to break us, this is not merely a way of speaking, nor is it only a doctrine. It is vital that we be broken by the Lord. It is not that the life of the Lord cannot cover the earth, but rather that His life is imprisoned by us. It is not that the Lord cannot bless the church, but that the Lord's life is so confined within us that there is no flowing forth. If the outward man remains unbroken, we can never be a blessing to His church, and we cannot expect the word of God to be blessed by Him through us!

The Alabaster Box Must Be Broken

The Bible tells of the pure spikenard. God purposely used this term "pure" in His word to show that it is truly spiritual. But if the alabaster box is not broken, the pure spikenard will not flow forth. Strange to say, many are still treasuring the alabaster box, thinking that its value exceeds that of the ointment. Many think that their outward man is more precious than their inward man. This becomes the problem in the church. One will treasure his cleverness, thinking he is quite important; another will treasure his own emotions, esteeming himself as an important person; others highly regard themselves, feeling they are better than others, their eloquence surpasses that of others, their quickness of action and exactness of judgment are superior, and so forth. However, we are not antique collectors; we are not vase admirers; we are those who desire to smell only the fragrance of the ointment. Without the breaking of the outward, the inward will not come forth. Thus individually we have no flowing out, but also the church does not have a living way. Why then should we hold ourselves as so precious, if our outward contains instead of releases the fragrance?

The Holy Spirit has not ceased working. One event after another, one thing after another, comes to us. Each disciplinary working of the Holy Spirit has but one purpose: to break our outward man so that our inward man may come through. Yet here is our difficulty: we fret over trifles, we murmur at small losses. The Lord is preparing a way to use us, yet scarcely has His hand touched us when we feel unhappy, even to the extent of quarreling with God and becoming negative in our attitude. Since being saved, we have been touched many times in various ways by the Lord, all with the purpose of breaking our outward man. Whether we are conscious of it or not, the aim of the Lord is to break this outward man.

So the Treasure is in the earthen vessel, but if the earthen vessel is not broken, who can see the Treasure within? What is the final objective of the Lord's working in our lives? It is to break this earthen vessel, to break our alabaster box, to crack open our shell. The Lord longs to find a way to bless the world through those who belong to Him. Brokenness is the way of blessing, the way of fragrance, the way of fruitfulness, but it is also a path sprinkled with blood. Yes, there is blood from many wounds. When we offer ourselves to the Lord to be at His service, we cannot afford to be lenient, to spare ourselves. We must allow the Lord utterly to crack our outward man, so that He may find a way for His out-working.

Each of us must find out for himself what is the mind of the Lord in his life. It is a most lamentable fact that many do not know what is the mind or intention of the Lord for their lives. How much they need for Him to open their eyes, to see that everything which comes into their lives can be meaningful. The Lord has not wasted even one thing. To understand the Lord's purpose, is to see very clearly that He is aiming at a single objective: the breaking of the outward man.

However, too many, even before the Lord raises a hand, are already upset. Oh, we must realize that all the experiences, troubles and trials which the Lord sends us are for our highest good. We cannot expect the Lord to give better things, for these are His best. Should one approach the Lord and pray, saying, "O Lord, please let me choose the best," I believe He would tell him, "What I have given you is the best; your daily trials are for your greatest profit." So the motive behind all the orderings of God is to break our outward man. Once this occurs and the spirit can come forth, we begin to be able to exercise our spirit.

The Timing in Our Brokenness

The Lord employs two different ways to break our outward man; one is gradual, the other sudden. To some, the Lord gives a sudden breaking followed by a gradual one. With others, the Lord arranges that they have constant daily trials, until one day He brings about large-scale breaking. If it is not the sudden first and then the gradual, then it is the gradual followed by the sudden. It would seem the Lord usually spends several years upon us before He can accomplish this work of breaking.

The timing is in His hand. We cannot shorten the time, though we certainly can prolong it. In some lives the Lord is able to accomplish this work after a few years of dealing; in others it is evident that after ten or twenty years the work is still unfinished. This is most serious! Nothing is more grievous than wasting God's time. How often the church is hindered! We can preach by using our mind, we can stir others by using our emotions; yet if we do not know how to use our spirit, the Spirit of God cannot touch people through us. The loss is great, should we needlessly prolong the time.

Therefore, if we have never before wholly and intelligently consecrated ourselves to the Lord, let us do so now, saying: "Lord, for the future of the church, for the future of the gospel, for Thy way, and also for my own life, I offer myself without condition, without reservation, into Thy hands. Lord, I delight to offer myself unto Thee and am willing to let Thee have Thy full way through me."

The Meaning of the Cross

Often we hear about the cross. Perhaps we are too familiar with the term. But what is the cross after all? When we really understand the cross we shall see it means the breaking of the outward man. The cross reduces the outward man to death; it splits open the human shell. The cross must break all that belongs to our outward man—our opinions, our ways, our cleverness, our self-love, our all. The way is clear, in fact crystal clear. As soon as our outward man is broken, our spirit can easily come forth. Consider a brother as an example. All who know him acknowledge that he has a keen mind, a forceful will, and deep emotions. But instead of being impressed by these natural characteristics of his soul, they realize they have met his spirit. Whenever people are fellowshipping with him, they encounter a spirit, a clean spirit. Why? Because all that is of his soul has been dealt with.

Take as another example, a sister. Those who know her recognize that she is of a quick disposition—quick in thought, quick of speech, quick to confess, quick in writing letters, and quick to tear up what she has written. However, those who meet her do not meet her quickness but rather her spirit. She is one who has been utterly broken and has become transparent. This breaking of the outward man is such a basic matter. We should not cling to our weak, soulish characteristics, still emitting the same fragrance even after five or ten years of the Lord's dealing with us. No, we must allow the Lord to forge a way in our lives.

Two Reasons for Not Being Broken

Why is it that after many years of dealing some remain the same? Some individuals have a forceful will; some have strong emotions; and others have a strong mind. Since the Lord is able to break these, why is it that after many years some are still unchanged? We believe there are two main reasons.

First, many who live in darkness are not seeing the hand of God. While God is working, while God is breaking, they do not recognize it as being from Him. They are devoid of light, seeing only men opposing them. They imagine their environment is just too difficult, that circumstances are to blame. So they continue in darkness and despair.

May God give us a revelation to see what is from His hand,

that we may kneel down and say to Him, "It is Thou; since it is Thou, I will accept." At least we must recognize *whose* hand it is that deals with us. It is not a human hand, nor our family's, not the brothers' and sisters' in the church, but God's. We need to learn how to kneel down and kiss the hand, love the hand that deals with us, even as Madame Guyon did. We must have this light to see that whatever the Lord has done, we accept and believe; the Lord can do no wrong.

Second, another great hindrance to the work of breaking the outer man is self-love. We must ask God to take away the heart of self-love. As He deals with us in response to our prayer, we should worship and say, "O Lord, if this be Thy hand, let me accept it from my heart." Let us remember that the one reason for all misunderstanding, all fretfulness, all discontent, it that we secretly love ourselves. Thus we plan a way whereby we can deliver ourselves. Many times problems arise due to our seeking a way of escape—an escape from the working of the cross.

He who has ascended the cross and refuses to drink the vinegar mingled with gall is the one who knows the Lord. Many go up to the cross rather reluctantly, still thinking of drinking vinegar mingled with gall to alleviate their pains. All who say, "The cup which the Father has given me, shall I not drink it?" will not drink the cup of vinegar mingled with gall. They can only drink of one cup, not two. Such as these are without any self-love. Self-love is a basic difficulty. May the Lord speak to us today that we may be able to pray: "O my God, I have seen that all things come from Thee. All my ways these five years, ten years, or twenty years, are of Thee. Thou hast so worked to attain Thy purpose, which is none other than that Thy life may be lived out through me. But I have been foolish. I did not see. I did many things to deliver myself, thus delaying Thy time. Today I see Thy hand. I am willing to offer myself to Thee. Once again I place myself in Thy hands."

Expect to See Wounds

There is no one more beautiful than one who is broken! Stubbornness and self-love give way to beauty in one who has been broken by God. We see Jacob in the Old Testament, how even in his mother's womb he struggled with his brother. He was subtle, tricky, deceitful. Yet his life was full of sorrows and grief. When a youth, he fled from home. For twenty years he was cheated by Laban. The wife of his heart's love, Rachel, died prematurely. The son of his love, Joseph, was sold. Years later Benjamin was detained in Egypt. He was successively dealt with by God, meeting misfortune after misfortune. He was stricken by God once, twice; indeed, his whole history could be said to be a history of being stricken by God. Finally after many such dealings, the man Jacob was transformed. In his last few years, he was quite transparent. How dignified was his answer to Pharaoh! How beautiful was his end, when he worshipped God on his staff! How clear were his blessings to his descendants! After reading the last page of his history, we want to bow our heads and worship God. Here is one who is matured, who knows God. Several decades of dealings have resulted in Jacob's outward man being broken. In his old age, the picture is a beautiful one.

Each of us has much of the same Jacob nature in us. Our only only hope is that the Lord may blaze a way out, breaking the outward man to such a degree that the inward man may come out and be seen. This is precious, and this is the way of those who serve the Lord. Only thus can we serve; only thus can we lead men to the Lord. All else is limited in its value. Doctrine does not have much use nor does theology. What is the use of mere mental knowledge of the Bible if the outward man remains unbroken? Only the person through whom God can come forth is useful.

After our outward man has been stricken, dealt with, and led through various trials, we have wounds upon us, thus allowing the spirit to emerge. We are afraid to meet some brothers and sisters whose whole being remains intact, never having been dealt with and changed. May God have mercy upon us in showing us clearly this way and in revealing to us that it is the only way. May He also show us that herein is seen the purpose of all His dealings with in these few years, say ten or twenty. Thus let no one despise the Lord's dealings. May He truly reveal to us what is meant by the breaking of the outward man. Should the outward man remain whole, everything would be merely in our mind, utterly useless. Let us expect the Lord to deal with us thoroughly.

Before and After

Brokenness

THE BREAKING of the outward man is the basic experience of all who serve God. This must be accomplished before He can use us in an effective way.

When one is working for God, two possibilities may arise. First, it is possible that with the outward man unbroken, one's spirit may be inert and unable to function. If he is a clever person, his mind governs his work; if he is a compassionate person, the emotions control his actions. Such work may appear successful but cannot bring people to God. Second, his spirit may come forth clad in his own thoughts or emotions. The result is mixed and impure. Such work will bring men into mixed and impure experience. These two conditions weaken our service to God.

If we desire to work effectively, we must realize that basically "it is the Spirit which quickens." Sooner or later — if not on the first day of our salvation, then perhaps ten years after — we must recognize this fact. Many have to be brought to their wits' end to see the emptiness of their labor before they know how useless are their many thoughts, their varied emotions. No matter how many people you can attract with your thoughts or emotions, the result comes to nothing. Eventually we must confess: "It is the Spirit which quickens." The Spirit alone makes people live. Your best thought, your best emotion cannot make people live. Man can be brought into life only by the Spirit. Many serving the Lord come to see this fact only after passing through much sorrow and many failures. Finally the Lord's word becomes meaningful to them: *that which quickens is the Spirit.* When the spirit is released then sinners may be born anew and saints may be established. When life is communicated through the channel of the spirit, those who receive it are born anew. When life is supplied through the spirit to believers, it results in their being established. Without the Spirit, there can be no new birth and no establishment.

One rather remarkable thing is that God does not mean to distinguish between His Spirit and our spirit. There are many places in the Bible where it is impossible to determine whether the word "spirit" indicates our human spirit or God's Spirit. Bible translators, from Luther down to present day scholars who have labored on the English versions, have been unable to decide if the word "spirit," as used in many places in the New Testament, refers to the human spirit or to the Spirit of God.

Of the whole Bible, Romans eight may very well be the chapter where the word "spirit" is used most frequently. Who can discern how many times the word "spirit" in this chapter refers to the human spirit and how many times to God's Spirit? In various English versions, the word "pneuma" (spirit) is sometimes written with a capital letter; other times, with a small letter. It is evident that these versions do not agree, and no one person's opinion is final. It is simply impossible to distinguish. When in regeneration we receive our new spirit, we receive God's Spirit too. The moment our human spirit is raised from the state of death, we receive the Holy Spirit. We often say that the Holy Spirit dwells in our spirit, but we find it hard to discern which is the Holy Spirit and which is our own spirit. The Holy Spirit and our spirit have become so mingled; while each is unique they are not easily distinguished.

Thus, the release of the spirit is the release of the human spirit as well as that of the Holy Spirit, Who is in the spirit of man. Since the Holy Spirit and our spirit are joined into one, (1 Cor. 6.17), they can be distinguished only in name, not in fact. And since the release of one means the release of both, others can touch the Holy Spirit whenever they touch our spirit. Thank God that inasmuch as you allow people to contact your spirit, you allow them to contact God. Your spirit has brought the Holy Spirit to man.

When the Holy Spirit is working, He needs to be carried by the human spirit. The electricity in an electric bulb does not travel like lightning. It must be conducted through electric wires. If you want to use electricity, you need an electric wire to bring it to you. In like manner, the Spirit of God employs the human spirit as His carrier, and through it He is brought to man.

Everyone who has received grace has the Holy Spirit dwelling in his spirit. Whether he can be used by the Lord depends not on his spirit but rather on his outward man. The difficulty with many is that their outward man has not been broken. There is not evident that blood-marked character — those wounds or scars. So God's Spirit is imprisoned within man's spirit and is not able to break forth. Sometimes our outward man is active, but the inward man remains inactive. The outward man has gone forth, while the inward man lags behind.

Some Practical Problems

Let us review this through some practical problems! Take preaching, for instance. How often we can be earnestly preaching — giving a well prepared, sound message — but inwardly feel as cold as ice. We long to stir others, yet we ourselves are unmoved. There is a lack of harmony between the outward and the inward man. The outward man is dripping from the heat, but the inward man is shivering from the cold. We can tell others how great the love of the Lord is, yet we are personally untouched by it. We can tell others how tragic is the suffering of the cross, yet upon returning to our room we can laugh. What can we do about this? Our mind may labor, our emotions may be energized, yet all the time one has the feeling that the inward man is merely observing the proceedings. The outward and the inward man are not one.

Consider another situation. The inward man is devoured by zeal. The person wants to shout, but he does not find utterance. After speaking for a long time, he still seems to be circling around. The more he is burdened within, the colder he becomes without. He longs to speak, but he cannot express himself. When he meets a sinner, his inward man feels like weeping, but he cannot shed a tear. There is a sense of urgency within him, yet when he ascends the pulpit and tries to shout, he finds himself lost in a maze of words. Such a situation is most trying. The root cause is the same: the outer shell still clings to him. The outward does not obey the dictates of the inward: inwardly crying, but outwardly unmoved; inwardly suffering, but outwardly untouched; full of thoughts within, but without, the mind a seeming blank. The spirit has yet to find a way to pierce the shell.

Thus the breaking of the outward man is the first lesson for everyone who would learn to serve God. He who is truly used by God is one whose outward thought and outward emotion do not act independently. If we have not learned this lesson, we shall find our effectiveness greatly impaired. May God bring us to the place where the outward man is completely broken.

When such a condition prevails, there will be an end to outward activity with inward inertness; an end to inward crying with outward composure; an end to an abundance of inner thoughts for which there is no utterance. You will not be poor in thought. You need not use twenty sentences to express what can be said in two. Your thoughts will assist instead of hinder your spirit.

Likewise, our emotions are also a very hard shell. Many who desire to be happy cannot express joy, or they may wish to weep yet cannot. If the Lord has stricken our outward man either through the discipline or the enlightening of the Holy Spirit, we are able to express joy or sorrow as is inwardly dictated. The release of the spirit makes it possible for us to abide increasingly in God. We touch the spirit of revelation in the Bible. Without effort our spirit can receive divine revelation. When we are witnessing or preaching, we send forth God's word through our spirit. Furthermore, we may most spontaneously contact the spirit in others by our spirit. Whenever one speaks in our presence, we can "size him up" —evaluate what kind of person he is, what attitude he is taking, what sort of Christian he is, and what his need is. Our spirit can touch his spirit. And what is wonderful, others easily contact our spirit. With some, we only meet their thoughts, their emotions, or their will. After conversing with them for hours, we still have not met the real person, though we may both be Christians. The outer shell is too thick for others to touch the inner man. With the breaking of the outward man, the spirit begins to flow and is ever open to others.

Launching Out and Retreating

Once the outward man is broken, man's spirit very naturally abides in the presence of God without ceasing. Two years after a certain brother trusted in the Lord, he read *The Practice of the Presence of God* by Brother Lawrence. After reading it, he felt grieved at his failure to abide unceasingly in the presence of God like Brother Lawrence. At that time he had hourly appointments to pray with someone. Why? Well, the Bible says, "Pray unceasingly," so they changed it to "Pray every hour." Every time they heard the clock strike the hour, they would pray. They exerted their utmost effort to retreat into God because they felt they could not maintain themselves in the continuous presence of God. It was as if they had slipped away while working and thus needed to retreat quickly back to God. Or they had projected themselves out while studying, and now they must withdraw swiftly to God. Otherwise they would find themselves away the whole day. They prayed often, spending whole days in prayer on the Lord's Day and half-days on Saturday. Thus they continued for two or three years. Nevertheless, the trouble remained: in withdrawing they enjoyed God's presence, but in going forth they lost it. Of course this is not their problem alone; such is the experience of many Christians. It indicates we are trying to maintain God's presence by our memory. The sense of His presence fluctuates according to our memory. When we remember, there is the consciousness of His presence; otherwise, there is none. This is sheer foolishness, for God's presence is in the spirit and not the memory.

To solve this problem, we must first settle the question of the breaking of the outward man. Since neither our emotion nor our thought has the same nature as God, it cannot be joined with Him. The Gospel of John chapter 4 shows us the nature of God. God is a Spirit. Our spirit alone is of the same nature as God; therefore, it can be eternally united with Him. If we try to get the presence of God by directing our thought, then when we are not concentrating, His presence seems to be lost. Again, if we seek to use our emotion to summon the presence of God, then as soon as our emotion relaxes, His presence seems to be gone. Sometimes we are happy, and we take this as having the presence of God. So when happiness ceases, the presence flees! Or we may assume that His presence is with us while we mourn and weep. Alas, we cannot shed tears all our life. Soon our tears will be dry, and then God's presence disappears. Both our thoughts and our emotions are human energies. All activity must come to an end. If we try to maintain God's presence with activity, then when the activity ceases, His presence ends. God's presence requires the sameness of nature. Only the inward man is of the same nature as God. Through it alone can His presence be manifested. When the outward man lives in activities, they can disturb the inward man. Thus the outward man is not a helper but a disturber. When the outward man is broken, the inward man enjoys peace before God.

Our spirit is given to us by God to enable us to respond to Him. But the outward man is ever responding to things without, hence depriving us of the presence of God. We cannot destroy all the things without, but we can break down the outward man. We cannot put a stop to all the things without; these millions and billions of things in the world are utterly beyond our control. Whenever anything happens, our outward man will respond; thus we are not able to enjoy God's presence in peace. We conclude, therefore, that experiencing the presence of God is contingent upon the breaking of our outward man.

If, through the mercy of God, our outward man has been broken, we may be characterized as follows: Yesterday we were full of curiosity, but today it is impossible to be curious. Formerly our emotions could be easily aroused, either stirring our love, the most delicate emotion, or provoking our temper, the crudest. But now no matter how many things crowd upon us, our inward man remains unmoved, the presence of God unchanged, and our inner peace unruffled.

It becomes evident that the breaking of the outward man is the basis for enjoying God's presence. Brother Lawrence was engaged in kitchen work. People were clamoring for things they wanted. Though there was the constant clatter of dishes and utensils, his inward man was not disturbed. He could sense God's presence in the hustle and bustle of a kitchen as much as in quiet prayer. Why? He was impervious to external noises. He had learned to commune in his spirit and ignore his soul life.

Some feel that to have God's presence their environment must be free of such distractions as the clatter of dishes. The farther away they are from mankind, the better they will be able to sense the presence of God. What a mistake! The trouble lies not in the dishes, nor in other people, but in themselves. God is not going to deliver us from the dishes; He will deliver us from our responses! No matter how noisy it is outside, the inside does not need to respond. Since the Lord has broken our outward man, we simply react as if we had not heard. Praise the Lord, we may possess very keen hearing, but due to the work of grace in our lives we are not at all influenced by the things pressing on our outward man. We can be before God on such occasions as much as when praying alone.

Once the outward man is broken, one no longer needs to retreat Godward, for he is always in the presence of God. Not so with one whose outward man is still intact. After running an errand he needs to return, for he assumes he has moved away from God. Even in doing the work of the Lord, he slips away from the One he serves. So it seems the best thing for him is not to make any move. Nevertheless, those that know God do not need to return, for they have never been away. They enjoy the presence of God when they set aside a day for prayer, and they enjoy the same presence in much the same degree when they are busily engaged in the menial tasks of life. Perhaps it is our common experience that in drawing near to God, we sense His presence; while if we are engaged in some activity, in spite of our vigilance, we feel that somehow we have drifted away. Suppose, for example, we are preaching the gospel or trying to edify people. After a while we feel like kneeling down to pray. But we have a sense that we must first retreat into God. Somehow our conversation with people has led us a little away from God, so in prayer we must first draw closer to Him. We have lost God's presence, so now we must have it restored to us. Or we may be occupied with some menial task such as scrubbing the floor. Upon completing our job, we decide to pray. Once again we feel we have taken a long trip and must return. What is the answer? The breaking of the outward man makes such returns unnecessary. We sense the presence of God in our conversation as much as in kneeling in prayer. Performing our menial tasks does not draw us away from God, hence we need not return.

Now let us consider an extreme case to illustrate this. Anger is the most violent of human feelings. But the Bible does not forbid us to be angry, for some anger is not related to sin. "Be angry but sin not," the Bible says. Nonetheless, anger of any kind is so strong it borders on sin. We do not find "Love but do not sin" nor "Be meek but do not sin" in God's word, because love and meekness are far removed from sin. But anger is close to sin. Perhaps a certain brother has committed a serious fault. He needs to be severely reprimanded. This is no easy matter. Rather would we exercise our feelings of mercy than bring our feelings of anger into play, for the latter can fall into something else with the least carelessness. Thus it is not easy to be properly angry according to the will of God. However, one who knows the breaking of the outward man can deal severely with another brother without his own spirit being disturbed or God's presence interrupted. He abides in God just as much in dealing with others as in prayer. Thus, after he has taken his brother to task, he can pray without any endeavor to retreat to God. We acknowledge that this is rather difficult; yet when the outward man is broken, such can well be the case.

The Dividing of the Outward and the Inward Man

When the outward man is broken, outside things will be kept outside, and the inward man will live before God continuously. The trouble with many is that their outward man and inward man are joined together, so what influences the outward influences the inward. Through the merciful working of God the outward man and inward man must be separated. Then what affects the outward will not be able to reach the inward. Though the outward man may be engaged in conversation, the inward man is fellowshipping with God. The outward may be burdened with listening to the clatter of dishes, yet the inward abides in God. One is able to carry on activities, to contact the world with the outer man, nevertheless the inner man remains unaffected because he still lives before God.

Consider an example or two. A certain brother is working on the road. If his outer and inner man have been divided, the latter will not be disturbed by outside things. He can labor in his outward man, while at the same time he is inwardly worshipping God. Or consider a parent: his outward man may be laughing and playing with his little child. Suddenly a certain spiritual need arises. He can at once meet the situation with his inward man, for he has never been absent from the presence of God. So it is important for us to realize that the dividing of the outward and inward man has a most decisive effect upon one's work and life. Only thus is one able to labor without distraction.

We can describe believers as either "single" or "dual" persons. With some their inner and outer man are one; with others the two have been separated. As long as one is a "single" person, he must summon his whole being into his work or into his prayer. In working he leaves God behind. In praying later, he must turn away from his work. Because his outward man has not been broken, he is forced to launch out and retreat. The "dual" person, on the other hand, is able to work with his outward man while his inward man remains constantly before God. Whenever the need arises, his inward man can break forth and manifest itself before others. He enjoys the unbroken presence of God. Let us ask ourselves, Am I a "single" or a "dual" person? Whether the outward man is divided from the inward does make all the difference.

If through the mercy of God you have experienced this dividing, then while you are working or are outwardly active, you know there is a man in you who remains calm. Though the outward man is engaged in external things, these will not penetrate into the inward man.

Here is the wondrous secret! Knowing the presence of God is through the dividing of these two. Brother Lawrence seemed to be busily occupied with kitchen work, yet within him there was another man standing before God and enjoying undisturbed communion with Him. Such an inner division will keep our reactions free from the contamination of flesh and blood.

In conclusion, let us remember that the ability to use our spirit depends upon the two-fold work of God: the breaking of the outward man and the dividing of spirit and soul, that is, the separating of our inward man from the outward. Only after God has carried out both of these processes in our lives are we able to exercise our spirit. *The outward man is broken through the discipline of the Holy Spirit; it is divided from the inward man by the revelation of the Holy Spirit (Heb. 4:12).*

Recognizing

"the Thing in Hand"

L ET ME FIRST explain our topic. Suppose a father asks his son to do a certain thing. The son answers, "Right now I have something in my hand; as soon as I finish it I will do what you order." "The thing in hand" is the thing which the son is doing prior to his father's orders. Immediately we recognize that we all have those "things in our hands" which hinder us in our walk with God. It might be anything—a good, important or seemingly necessary thing—which preoccupies us and diverts our attention. As long as the outward man remains unbroken, we shall most likely find our hands full of things. Our outward man has its own religious interests, appetites, concerns and labors. So when the Spirit of God moves in our spirit, our outward man cannot answer God's call. Thus it is the "thing in hand" which blocks the way to spiritual usefulness.

The Limited Strength of the Outward Man

Our human strength is limited. If a brother can only carry fifty pounds, and you want him to take an additional ten, he simply cannot do it. He is a limited person, unable to do unlimited work. The fifty pounds he is already carrying is "the thing in hand". As the physical strength of our outermost man is limited, so it is with the strength of our outward man.

Many, not realizing this principle, carelessly spend the strength of their outward man. If, for example, one lavished all his love upon his parents, he would have no strength left for loving his brothers, not to mention others. In thus exhausting his (soul) strength, there is nothing left to direct to others.

So it is with our mental strength. If one's attention is focused on a certain matter, and he exhausts all his time in thinking about it, he will have no strength to think of other matters. In His word, God has explained our problem: "The law of the Spirit of life in Christ Jesus has set me free from the law of sin and of death" (Rom. 8:2). But why is this law of the Spirit of life ineffectual in certain people? Again we read: "The righteous requirement of the law should be fulfilled in us who walk . . . according to Spirit" (Rom. 8:4). In other words, the law of the Spirit of life works effectively only for those who are spiritual, that is, those who mind the things of the Spirit. Who are these? Those who do not mind the things of the flesh. The word "mind" in verse 5 can also be translated "to be intent upon, to be attentive to." For instance, a mother is going out and she leaves her baby in the care of a friend. To take care of the baby means to be attentive to him. When you are entrusted with the care of a baby, you dare not be distracted to do other things. Similarily, only those who are not intent on carnal things can be attentive to spiritual things. Those who are intent upon spiritual things come under the force of the law of the Holy Spirit. Our mental strength is limited. If we exhaust it on the things of the flesh, we shall find ourselves mentally inadequate for the things of the Spirit.

We realize, then, that just as our physical strength is limited, so is it with the soul strength of our outward man. As long as we have "things in hand" we cannot do God's work. According to the number of things in hand, strength for serving God decreases or increases. Hence the thing in hand becomes indeed a hindrance, and no small one.

Again, one may have many things in hand emotionally: such as varied and conflicting likes or dislikes, inclinations or expectations. All these pull with a magnetic attraction. With so many things in hand, when God asks a person for his affection he cannot respond, for he has already used up all his emotion. If he has exhausted a two-day supply of emotional resources, it will be that long before he can adequately feel and speak again. Thus when emotion is wasted on lesser things it cannot be used unrestrictedly for God.

Then there is someone manifesting an iron will, a strong personality whose volitional powers seem unlimited. Yet in the things of God he seems unable to make up his mind; how often the strongest person will waver in his decisions before God. Why is this? Before we answer let us consider another who is full of ideas. Though he never seems at a loss conceiving new schemes, when it comes to discerning the will of God in spiritual things he is utterly void of light. Why is this so?

While the outward man is so weighed down with the things in hand and is so exhausted, there is little strength left for any spiritual exercise. It is needful, then, to see the limited strength of the outer man. Even though it is broken there must be a wisdom in using this strength. How necessary, then, to have "empty hands"!

The Spirit's Use of a Broken Outward Man

In His dealing with man, God's Spirit never by-passes man's spirit. Nor can our spirit by-pass the outer man. This is a most important principle to grasp. As the Holy Spirit does not pass over man's spirit in His working in man, no more does our spirit ignore the outward man and function directly. In order to touch other lives, our spirit must pass through the outward man. Hence, when the latter's strength is consumed by the many things in hand, God cannot do His work through us. There is no outlet for the human spirit nor for the Holy Spirit. The inward man cannot come forth because he is resisted and blocked by the outward man. That is why we have repeatedly suggested that this outward man must be broken.

The thing in hand is there before God begins to work. It does not belong to God, nor does it need His order, power, or decision to be carried out. It is not something under the hand of God but rather an independent action.

Before your outward man is broken you are occupied with your own things, walk in your own way, and love your own people. If God wants to use your love in loving the brethren, He must first break your outward man. This love of yours is thereby enlarged. The inward man must love, but he has to love through the outward man. If the outward man is occupied with the thing in hand, the inward is deprived of its proper channel for loving.

Again, when the inward man needs to use his will, he finds it is acting independently, already engaged by the thing in hand. To break our will, God must strike us a heavy blow until we prostrate ourselves in the dust and say, "Lord, I dare not think, I dare not ask, I dare not decide on my own. In each and every thing I need Thee." In our being stricken, we must learn that our will is not to act independently. Only then is our will ready to be used by the inward man.

Without the cooperation of the outward man, the inward is most handicapped. Suppose a brother is going to preach the Word. He has a burden in his spirit. However, if he fails to find corresponding thoughts, he cannot release his burden and it will soon fade away. Even though the burden may permeate his whole spirit, all is futile if his mind is unable to communicate it.

We cannot bring men to salvation merely with the burden in our spirit; this must be expressed through our mind. The burden within must be coordinated with the mouth without. Without utterance it is impossible to make known to others the word of God. Man's words are not God's word, but the latter must be communicated by the former. When man has God's words, God can speak; when he does not, God cannot speak. The trouble today is that our inward man is available to God—able to receive God's burden—but our outward man is driven by such multitudinous, confusing thoughts from morning till night that our spirit can find no outlet.

Thus it is that God must crush our outward man. He breaks our will by taking away the things in our will's "hand" so that it cannot act independently. Not that we have no mind, but that we do not think after the flesh, according to our wandering imaginations. Not that we are devoid of emotion, but that all our emotions are under the control and restraint of the inward man. This gives the inner man a will, a mind, and emotions that are usable. God wants our spirit to use our outward man in loving, in thinking, and in deciding. While it is not His thought to annihilate our outward man, we must receive this basic experience of being broken if we aspire to effectually serve God.

Until this happens, the inward and the outward man are at odds with each other, each acting independently of the other. When we are broken, the outward man is brouder control of the inward, thus unifying our personality so that the shattered outward man may be a channel for the inward man.

Now it must be recognized that a unified personality may often characterize an unsaved person, but in this case the inward man is under control of the outward man. Though the human spirit exists, it is so beaten by the outward man that it can at best only raise some conscientious protests. The inward man is utterly dominated by the outward man.

However, after one is saved, it is God's intention that he should experience a reversal of this order. As much as his outward man controlled the inward before he was saved, so now his inward man should hold absolute sway over the outward.

We can use bicycling as an illustration. On *flat* ground, we pedal the bicycle and the wheels roll along the road. Similarly, when our inward man is strong and the outward man is broken, we "pedal" and the "wheels" roll along the road. We can decide whether to continue or stop and how fast to go. In the case of a bicycle on a *down* slope however, the wheels rotate without any pedaling at all, for the road just seems to urge us along. In like manner, if our outward man is hard and unbroken, it will be like a bicycle coasting out of control down an incline. Should the Lord be gracious to us and level out the slope of our experience by breaking the outward man—so that he can no longer give counsel and make decisions independently— we shall be as those who are able to properly use their spirit.

The Person Broken, Not Just Taught

No one is equipped to work simply because he has learned some teachings. The basic question is still: What kind of man is he? Can one whose inner workings are wrong, but whose teaching is right, supply the need of the church? The basic lesson we must learn is to be transformed into a vessel fit for the Master's use. This can only be done by the breaking of the outward man.

God is at work in our lives unceasingly. Many years of sufferings, trials, hindrances—this is the hand of God, daily seeking to carry on His work of breaking us. Do you not see what God is doing in this endless round of difficulties? If not, you should ask Him; "O God, open my eyes that I may see Thy hand." How often the eyes of an ass are sharper than those of a self-styled prophet.

Though the ass had already seen the Angel of the Lord, its master had not. The ass recognized the forbidding hand of God, but the self-styled prophet did not. We should be aware that brokenness is God's way in our lives. How sad that some still imagine that if they could only absorb more teaching, accumulate more preaching material, and assimilate more Bible exposition, they would be profitable to God. This is absolutely wrong. God's hand is upon you to break you—not according to your will, but His; not according to your thoughts, but His; not according to your decision, but His. Our difficulty is that as God withstands us, we blame others. We react like that prophet who, blind to God's hand, blamed the ass for refusing to budge.

All that comes to us is ordered by God. To a Christian, nothing is accidental. We should ask God to open our eyes that we may see that He is striking us in all things and in all areas of our life. One day, when by His grace upon us we are able to accept the ordering of God in our environment, our spirit will be released and ready to function.

One Law Which Is Unaffected by Prayer

There is an immutable law of God's working in us: His specific purpose is breaking us and releasing our spirit for free exercise. We must understand that none of our praying, pleading or promising will affect or change this purpose. It is according to His law of accomplishing a brokenness and release in us; all our praying will not alter this law. If you deliberately thrust your hand into the fire, will prayer keep you free from scorching and pain (barring a miracle)? If you do not wish to be scorched by fire yet you deliberately thrust your hand into it anyway, then do not think that prayer will save you from the consequences; it will not. In like manner, let us see that God's dealing with us is deliberate, according to His law. In order to come forth, the inward man must pass through the outward. Until our outward man is shattered, the inward simply cannot come forth. Do not try to overturn this law and its effects by praying for blessings; such prayers are in vain. Praying can never change God's law.

We must settle this once and for all. The way of spiritual

work lies in God's coming out through us. This is the only way God has ordained. To one who is unbroken, the gospel is blocked and cannot flow out through the life. Let us bow low before God. To obey God's law is far better than saying many prayers. It is much better to stop praying and confess: "God, I prostrate myself before Thee." Yes, how often our prayers for blessings are actually raising up barriers. We long for blessing, yet seem to find God's mercy in crushing experiences. If only we would seek for enlightenment, learn to submit ourselves to His hand, and obey His law, we would find that the outcome is the very blessing we long for.

How to Know Man

TO KNOW MAN is vital to a worker. When someone comes to us, we must discern his spiritual condition, his nature, and the extent of his spiritual progress. We must determine whether he has said what is really in his heart and how much he has left unsaid. Further, we should perceive his characteristics — whether he is hard or humble, whether his humility is true or false. Our effectiveness in service is closely related to our discernment of man's spiritual condition. If God's Spirit enables us through our spirit to know the condition of the person before us, we can then impart the appropriate word.

In the Gospels we find that whenever men came to our Lord, He always had the right word. This is a marvelous thing. The Lord did not talk to the Samaritan woman about new birth, nor did he tell Nicodemus of living water. The truth of the new birth was for Nicodemus, while the truth of the living water was for the Samaritan woman. How appropriate they were. Those who had not followed Him were invited to come; but those who desired to follow Him were invited to bear the cross. To one who volunteered, He spoke of counting the cost; while to one who lingered, He said "Let the dead bury their dead." Our Lord's words were most appropriate, *for He knew all men.* Our Lord knew whether they came as earnest seekers or merely to spy on Him; and what He said to them was always right to the point. May God be merciful to us that we also may learn from Him how to know man so that we may be effective in dealing with people. Without such imparted knowledge, a brother can only handle souls by his own understanding. If he has a special feeling on a certain day, he will speak to everybody according to that feeling, no matter who it is that comes. If he has a favorite subject, he speaks on it to all who come to him. How can such work be effective? No physician can use the same prescription for all his patients. Alas, some who serve God have only one prescription. Though they cannot first diagnose people's sicknesses, they are trying to cure them. In spite of their ignorance of man's complexities and their lack of insight into man's spiritual condition, none the less they seem to be quite ready to treat every ailment. How foolish to have only one spiritual prescription, yet try to meet every kind of spiritual disease!

Have you imagined that it is the dull who cannot discern, and only the clever who can? No, in this work the clever and the dull are equally excluded. You cannot use your (independent) mind or feeling to discern people. No matter how keen your mind, you cannot penetrate the depth of man and reveal his condition.

After meeting a soul, each worker must first discern what that individual's real need is before God. Often you cannot depend on what he says. Though he may correctly insist that he has a "headache," this may be only a symptom of a deeper condition whose roots are to be found elsewhere. Just because he feels warm does not necessarily mean he has a "high fever." He is likely to tell you many things which have no bearing on his case. A "sick person" seldom understands his real trouble; so he needs you to diagnose for him and offer the means of cure. You may want him to tell you his need, but he is prone to be mistaken. Only a trained diagnostician who is skilled in recognizing spiritual ailments, can discern the "patient's" real need. In every diagnosis you must have certainty. One who is merely subjective is sure to afflict people with imaginative illnesses, stubbornly insisting that this or that is what ails them.

Sometimes we may discover that the particular trouble is beyond our ability to help. Do not be so foolish as to assume you can cope with every situation and help all. For those whom you *can* help, you should spend and be spent. When you *cannot* be of help, you should tell the Lord, "This is beyond my ability; I cannot discern this disease. I haven't learned this yet. O Lord, be merciful." We should never think we can handle all the spiritual work or try to monopolize it. Here is our chance to see the supply of the different members of the Body. If you feel a certain brother or sister can handle the trouble, seek him out and say, "This is beyond my measure; perhaps this is in your jurisdiction." In this way of working together in the Body, we learn to act relatedly, not independently.

We must emphasize it again: every worker must learn before the Lord how to *know* man. How many lives are spoiled after passing through the hands of eager brothers who have not learned, but vainly give subjective views to meet objective needs! People are not necessarily afflicted with ailments that we imagine they have. Our responsibility is to discern their true spiritual condition. If we have not first been a partaker of spiritual understanding how can we hope to help the rest of God's children?

We Are His Instrumentality

In diagnosing a case, a medical doctor has recourse to many medical instruments. This is not so with us. We have no thermometer nor x-ray, nor any other such device to help us discern man's spiritual condition. How, then, do we discern whether a brother is spiritually ill or determine the nature of his trouble? It is wonderful that God has designed us to be as "thermometers" for measuring. By His working in our lives, He would equip us to discern what "ails" a person. As the Lord's spiritual "doctors" we must have a thorough inward preparation. We must be deeply conscious of the weight of our responsibility.

Suppose the thermometer had never been invented. The doctor would have to determine whether his patient had a fever by the mere touch of his hand. His hand would serve as the thermometer. How sensitive and accurate his hand would need to be! In spiritual work, this is exactly the case.

We are the thermometers, the instrumentalities. We must undergo thorough training and strict discipline, for whatever is untouched in us will be left untouched in others. Moreover, we cannot help others to learn lessons which we ourselves have not learned before God. The more thorough our training, the greater will be our usefulness in God's work. Likewise the more we spare ourselves — our pride, our narrowness, our happiness — the less our usefulness. If we have covered these things in ourselves, we cannot uncover them in others. A proud person cannot deal with another with the same condition; a hypocrite cannot touch the hypocrisy in another, nor can one who is loose in his life have a helpful effect on one who suffers the same difficulty. How well we know that if such is still in our nature we will not be able to condemn such particular sin in others; we in fact can hardly recognize it in others. A doctor may cure others without curing himself, but this can hardly be true in the spiritual realm. The worker is himself first a patient; he must be healed before he can heal others. What he has not seen he cannot show others. Where he has not trodden he cannot lead others. What he has not learned he cannot teach others.

We must see that we are the instruments prepared by God for knowing man. Hence we must be dependable, qualified to give an accurate diagnosis. That my feelings may be reliable, I need to pray, "O Lord, do not let me go untouched, unbroken and unprepared." I must allow God to work in me what I have never dreamed of, so that I may become a prepared vessel whom He can use. A doctor would not use a defective thermometer. How much more serious it is for us to touch spiritual conditions than physical illnesses while still retaining our own thoughts, emotions, opinions and ways. If we still want to do this, and then suddenly want to do that, we are yet unstable. How can we be used when we are so undependable? We must pass through God's dealings or our efforts are vain.

Then again, we must face this question. Are we really conscious of the greatness of our responsibility? God's Spirit does not work directly in people; He does His work through man. People's needs are met on the one hand by the discipline of the Holy Spirit (in ordering their environment), and on the other by the ministry of the Word. Without the supply of the ministry of the Word, the spiritual problem of the saints cannot be solved. What responsibility has fallen upon His workers! It is most serious. Whether or not one is usable determines the supply of the church.

Suppose it is characteristic of a certain illness to reach a temperature of, say, 103°F. But unless you know the exact temperature, your diagnosis cannot be certain. You cannot determine by touching the patient with your hand that he has a fever of about 103°. Even so in the spiritual, it would be too risky for us to try to help others while our feelings and opinions are all wrong and our spiritual understanding is inadequate. Only if we are accurate and trustworthy can the Spirit of God be released through us.

The starting point of a spiritual work is marked by many readjustments made before God. A thermometer is made according to a definite standard and is carefully examined to meet rigid specifications. If, then, we are the thermometer, how strict must be the discipline to bring us up to God's standard of accuracy! In God's work we are "doctors" as well as "medical instruments." How important it is that we pass His test.

The Key to Perceiving the Patient's Spirit

In knowing a patient's condition, we should consider both the patient's side and our side. If you want to know what ails a person, you need first to recognize his most prominent feature. It will stand out so conspicuously that, try as he may, he cannot hide it. A proud person will reveal pride. With a sad person, a note of sadness pervades even his laughter. Invariably, the nature of the person will cause a certain definite impression to be felt.

There are many references in the Bible describing different types of spirit. Some people are hasty of spirit; others are hardened in their spirit; still others have a sorrowful spirit. We can say one has a haughty spirit, another has a depressed spirit, and so forth. Whence come these different conditions of the spirit? For instance, in a hard spirit, where does the hardness come from? In a proud spirit, whence comes the haughtiness? Surely our human spirit in its normal state is not tinged with anything. It is designed just to manifest the Spirit of God. How can it be, then, that the spirit is spoken of as hard, or proud, or haughty, or unforgiving, or jealous? The answer is this: the outward and inward man are not divided, and thus the condition of the outward man becomes that of the inward. The spirit is hard because it is clothed in the hardness of the outward man, or proud because it is clothed with the pride of the outward man, or jealous because of the jealousy of the outward man. Originally the spirit is neutral in nature but it can take on the character of the outward man if the latter is not broken.

Our spirit emanates from God. Thus originally it is pure, before it is affected by the impure state of the outward man. But it becomes proud or hard wholly because of the unbrokenness of the outward man. How the condition of the outward man will taint the spirit so as to come forth with the spirit! Thus to purify the spirit, one must deal not with the spirit, but with the outward man. We must realize that the trouble lies not with the spirit but with the outward man. From the kind of spirit flowing forth we can detect immediately wherein a man has not been broken. The particular condition of the outward man stands revealed in the type of spirit we contact.

Once we have learned to touch man's spirit we know exactly what is his need. This secret of knowing man is by touching his spirit — in sensing what it is clothed with. Let us repeat emphatically that this is the basic principle for knowing another man: by sensing, or touching his spirit. As the spirit flows forth it reveals the nature of the outward man as to whether the latter has been broken or not, for our spirit takes its color from the outward man as it flows forth.

When one is strong in a particular point, it is like a thing which stands out before you. Just to reach out is to touch it. If you feel, you will know what it is. You will realize that this thing is his unbroken outward man. If you can thus sense a man's spirit, you will know his condition. You will know what is revealed by him or what he is trying to conceal. So we say again, if you want to know man, you must know him according to his spirit.

Our Own Preparation for Knowing Man

Let us now consider our part in knowing man. The disciplinary measures the Holy Spirit takes with us are God-given lessons by which, in one thing after another, we are broken. It takes many breakings in many areas of our lives for us to attain to a place of usefulness. When we say we can touch another through the spirit, it does not mean that we can similarly touch all individuals nor that we can discern another's spiritual condition in totality. It is simply that in the particular thing where we have been disciplined by the Holy Spirit and broken by the Lord, we can touch another. If in a particular thing we have not been broken by the Lord, we can in no wise supply that need to our brother. At that very point our spirit is insensitive and impotent.

This is an invariable spiritual fact! Our spirit is released according to the degree of our brokenness. The one who has accepted the most discipline is the one who can best serve. The more one is broken, the more sensitive he is. The more loss one has suffered, the more he has to give. Wherever we desire to save ourselves, in that very thing we become spiritually useless. Whenever we preserve and excuse ourselves, at that point we are deprived of spiritual sensitivity and supply. Let no one imagine he can be effective and disregard this basic principle.

Only those who have learned can serve. You may learn ten years' lessons'in one year or take twenty or thirty years to learn one year's lessons. Any delay in learning means a delay in serving. If God has put a desire in your heart to serve Him, you should understand what is involved. The way of service lies in brokenness, in accepting the discipline of the Holy Spirit. The measure of your service is determined by the degree of discipline and brokenness. Be assured that human emotion or cleverness cannot help. How much you really possess is based upon how much God has wrought in your life. Therefore, the more you are dealt with, the keener is your perception of man. The more you are disciplined by the Holy Spirit, the more readily your spirit can touch another.

It is very important to remember that while God's Spirit is given to us believers once for all, we in our spirit must go on learning throughout life. Thus the more we learn, the more we can discern. It is a source of grief to us that so many brothers and sisters in the Lord do not know how to exercise spiritual discernment. Too many fail to differentiate between what is of the Lord and what is of human nature. Only as we have experienced the Lord's strict dealing with us in a certain matter can we quickly detect even the initial sprouting in others. We do not need to wait for its fruit. We can discern long before harvest time. So our spiritual sensitivity is gradually gained through experiencing God's hand upon us. For example, someone may mentally condemn pride, yes, even preach against it, yet not sense the sinfulness of pride in his own spirit. Thus when pride appears in his brother, his spirit is not distressed; it may even be sympathetic. Then the day comes when God's Spirit so works in his life that he really sees what pride is. He is dealt with by God, and his pride is consumed. Though his preaching against pride may sound the same as before, yet now every time a spirit of pride appears in his brother, he senses its ugliness and is distressed. What he has learned and seen from God enables him to sense and to be distressed. ("Distress" most suitably describes such an inward sensitivity.) Now that he recognizes this ailment, he can serve his brother. Once he was attacked by the same affliction; now he is cured. (This does not imply that he should claim complete deliverance — simply that he knows some measure of cure.) This is how we come to spiritual knowledge.

Spiritual sensitivity comes about only through many dealings. Are we really profited if we preserve ourselves? "For whosoever shall save his life shall lose it." We must ask the Lord not to withdraw His hand from us. How tragic not to recognize what the Lord is doing. We may even be unwittingly resisting His hand. The absence of spiritual understanding is due to the lack of spiritual learning. Therefore, let us realize that the more we are dealt with, the more we shall know men and things, and the more we can supply others' needs. There is no other way to enlarge the sphere of service; we must broaden the scope of our experiences.

Learning to Practice This

Once these basic lessons have been learned, we find our spirit is released and able to pinpoint the real condition of others. How can we put this into practice?

To touch man's spirit we must wait till he opens his mouth and talks. Few ever arrive at the place where they can touch man's spirit without first hearing what he has to say. The word of God says: "For out of the abundance of the heart the mouth speaks" (Matthew 12:34). Whatever his real intention may be, his spirit is revealed by what his mouth speaks. If he is haughty, a haughty spirit will manifest itself; if hypocritical, a hypocritical spirit will be evident; or if envious, a jealous spirit. As you listen to him speak, you can touch his spirit. Do not merely pay attention to what he says but especially note his spirit's condition. We really know man not by his words alone, but by his spirit.

On one occasion when the Lord Jesus was traveling toward Jerusalem, two of the disciples saw that the Samaritans did not receive Him. They questioned Him: "Lord wilt Thou that we command fire to come down from heaven and consume them as also Elias did?" (Luke 9:54). As they were speaking, their spirit was revealed. The Lord's reply was, "Ye know not of what spirit ye are" (9:55). The Lord shows us here that to listen to man's words is to know his spirit. As soon as the words are uttered, the spirit is revealed, "for out of the abundance of the heart the mouth speaks."

There is yet another point to bear in mind. When you are listening to a conversation, do not allow the topic under discussion to distract you from the spirit. Suppose two brothers are involved in a quarrel, each one blaming the other. If this matter is brought to you, how are you to deal with it? Although you may have no objective way of checking the facts if only the two are present, you do know that, as soon as they open their mouths, their spirits are revealed. Among Christians, right or wrong is judged not only by action but also by the spirit. When a brother starts to talk, you may sense immediately that his spirit is wrong, though you may lack factual information in the case. One brother may complain that the other scolded him, but immediately you sense his spirit is not right! The real issue is with the spirit.

Before God, right or wrong is determined not so much by the deed as by the spirit. How often in the church a wrong deed is accompanied by a wrong spirit. But if judgment is made solely according to the deed, we have dragged the church into another realm. We should be in the realm of the spirit, not in that of mere outward action.

Once our own spirit has been released, we can detect the condition of others' spirits. If we contact a spirit which is closed, we have to exercise our spirit in judging the issue and discerning the man. May we be able to say with Paul, "We henceforth know no one according to flesh" (2 Cor. 5:16). We do not know man according to flesh, but according to spirit. Having learned this basic lesson, we provide a way for God to work out His purpose.

The Church
and God's Work

IF WE REALLY UNDER-
STAND the nature of God's
work, we shall readily admit that the outward man is truly a
formidable hindrance. It is true to say that God is much
restricted by man. The people of God should know the
ultimate purpose of the church and also the inter-
relationships among the church, God's power, and God's
work.

God's Manifestation and God's Restriction

There came a time when God committed Himself to
human form—in the person of Jesus of Nazareth. Before
the Word became flesh, God's fullness knew no bounds.
However, once the incarnation became a reality, His work
and His power were limited to this flesh. Will this Man,
Christ Jesus, restrict or manifest God? We are shown by the
Bible that, far from limiting God, He has wonderfully manifested God's fullness. **The fullness of God is the fullness
of this flesh.**

In our day God commits Himself to the church. His power and His work are in the church. Just as in the Gospels we find all God's work given to the Son, so today God has entrusted all His works to the church and will not act apart from it. From the Day of Pentecost up to the present, God's work has been carried out through the church. Think of the church's trememdous responsibility. God's committal to the church is like His committal previously to one Man, Christ—without reservation or restriction. But the church may restrict God's work or limit His manifestation.

Jesus of Nazareth is God Himself. His whole being from within to without is to reveal God. His emotions reflect God's emotions; His thoughts reveal God's thoughts. While on this earth He could say; "Not that I should do My will, but the will of Him that has sent Me . . . . The Son can do nothing of Himself save whatever He sees the Father doing . . . For I have not spoken from Myself, but the Father who sent Me has Himself given Me commandment what I should say and what I should speak" (John 6:38; 5:19; 12:49). Here we see a Man to whom God is committed. He is the Word that became flesh. He is God becoming man. He is perfect. When the day came that God desired to distribute His life to men, that Man could declare: ". . . The grain of wheat falling into the ground . . . if it die . . . bears much fruit" (John 12:24). Thus God has chosen the church to be His vessel today—the vessel of His speaking, for the manifestation of His power and of His working.

The basic teaching of the Gospels is the presence of God in one Man, while that of the Epistles is God in the church. May our eyes be opened to the glorious fact: God formerly dwelt in the Man Jesus Christ, but now God is only in the church, not in any other thing.

When this light dawns on us, we will spontaneously lift up our eyes to heaven saying, "O, God! How much we have hindered Thee!" In Christ, the Almighty God was still almighty without suffering any restriction or straitening. What God expects today is that this same power may remain intact as He resides in the church. He should be as free in manifesting Himself in the church as He was in Christ. Any restriction or disability in the church will invariably limit God. This is a most serious thing; we do not mention it lightly. The hindrance in each of us constitutes a hindrance to God.

Why is the discipline of the Holy Spirit so important? Why is the dividing of spirit and soul so urgent? It is because God must have a way through us. Let no one think that we are only interested in individual spiritual experience. Our concern is God's way and His work. Is God free to work through our lives? Unless we are dealt with and broken through discipline, we shall restrict God. Without the breaking of the outward man, the church cannot be a channel for God.

Breaking—God's Way of Working

Let us now proceed to consider how the breaking of the outward man will affect our reading of God's word, our being ministers of His word, and our preaching the gospel.

(1) **Reading the Bible:** It is beyond question that what we *are* determines what we get out of the Bible. How often man in his conceit relies on his unrenewed and confused mind to read the Bible. The fruit is nothing but his own thought. He does not touch the spirit of the Holy Scriptures. It we expect to meet the Lord in His word, our thoughts must first be broken by God. We may think highly of our cleverness, but to God it is a great obstacle. It can never lead us into God's thought.

There are at least two basic requirements for reading the Bible: first, our thought must enter into the thought of the Bible; and second, our spirit must enter into the spirit of the Bible. You must think as the writer—whether Paul, Peter or John—when he is writing God's word. Your thought must begin where his thought begins, and develop as his develops. You must be able to reason as he reasons and to exhort as he exhorts. In other words, your thought must be geared to his thought. This will allow the Spirit to give you the precise meaning of the Scriptures.

Think of a person coming to the Bible with his mind already set. He reads the Bible to get support for his preconceived doctrines. How tragic! An experienced person, after hearing such a one speak for five or ten minutes, can discern whether the speaker is using the Bible for his own ends or if his thought has entered into the thought of the Bible. There is a difference in realm here. One may stand up and give a pleasing, seemingly scriptural message, but actually his thought is contradictory to the thought of the Bible. Or we may hear someone preach whose thought expresses the thought of the Bible and is therefore harmonious and united with it. Though this condition should be the norm, not all reach it. To unite our thought with the thought of the Bible, we need to have the outward man broken. Do not think our Bible reading is poor because of a lack of instruction. The defect is rather in us because our thoughts have not been subdued by God. So to be broken is to cease from our own activities and from our subjective thinking, and gradually to begin to touch the mind of the Lord and follow the trend of thought of the Bible. Not until the outward man is broken, can we enter into the thought of God's word.

Now while this is important, we have yet to mention the primary matter. The Bible is more than words, ideas and thoughts. The most outstanding feature of the Bible is that God's Spirit is released through this Book. When a writer, whether Peter, John, Matthew or Mark, is inspired by the Holy Spirit, his renewed mind follows the inspired thought and his spirit is released with the Holy Spirit. The world cannot understand that there is a spirit in God's word, and that that spirit can be released just as it is manifested in prophetic ministry. Today if you are listening to a prophetic message, you will realize that there is a mystical something other than word and thought present. This you can clearly sense, and may well call it the spirit in God's word.

There is not only *thought* in the Bible; the *spirit itself* comes forth. Thus, it is only when your spirit can come out and touch the spirit of the Bible that you can understand what the Bible says. To illustrate, let us think of a naughty boy who deliberately breaks a neighbor's window. The neighbor comes out and gives him quite a tongue-lashing. When the boy's mother learns of the mischief, she also rebukes him severely. But somehow there is a difference in spirit between the two scoldings. The one is ill-tempered, given in an angry spirit; the other expresses love, hope, and training, This is just a simple example. The Spirit who inspires the writing of the Scriptures is the eternal Spirit, ever present in the Bible. If our outward man has been broken, our spirit is released and can touch that Spirit who inspires the Scriptures. Otherwise, the Bible will remain as a dead book in our hands.

(2) **Ministry of the Word:** God desires that we understand His word, for this is the starting point of spiritual service. He is equally anxious to put His word as a burden in our spirit so that we may use it to minister to the church. In Acts 6:4 we read, "But we will give ourselves up to prayer and the ministry of the word." "Ministry" means serving. So the ministry of the word means serving people with the word of God.

In ministry what is our difficulty that we fail to release the word within us? Often one may be heavily burdened with a word which he feels he must communicate to the brethren. However, as he stands to speak sentence after sentence, the inner burden remains as heavy as ever. Even after an hour has passed, there is no sense of relief, and finally he must leave as heavily burdened as when he came. Why? It is because his outward man has not been broken. Instead of being a help, the soul faculties become an obstacle to the inward man.

Yet once the outward man is broken, utterance is no longer a problem. One can then think of appropriate words to express his inner feeling. Through release, the inner burden is lightened. This is the way to minister God's word to the church. So we repeat: the outward man is the greatest hindrance to the ministry of the word of God.

Many have the erroneous notion that clever people are best able to be used. How wrong! No matter how clever you are, the outward can never substitute for the inward man. Only after the outward man is broken can the inward find adequate thought and appropriate words. The shell of the outward man must be smashed by God. The more it is shattered, the more the life in the spirit is released. As long as this shell remains intact, the burden in the spirit cannot be released nor can God's life and power flow from you to the church. It is mostly through the ministry of God's word that His life and power are supplied. Unless your inward man is released, people can only hear your voice; they cannot touch life. You may have a word to give, but others fail to receive; you have no means of utterance.

The difficulty is that the life within fails to flow out. There is a word of God going on within, yet it cannot be manifested because of the obstacle without. God does not have a free way in you.

(3) Preaching the Gospel: There is a common misconception that people believe the gospel because they have been either mentally convinced of the doctrinal correctness or emotionally stirred by its appeal. In actual fact, those who respond to the gospel for either of these two reasons do not last long. Intellect and emotion need to be reached, but these alone are insufficient. Mind may reach mind and emotion may reach emotion, but salvation probes much deeper. Spirit must touch spirit. Only when the spirit of the preacher blossoms forth and shines do sinners fall down and capitulate to God. This is the proper spirit necessary in preaching the gospel.

A miner greatly used by God wrote a book called *Seen and Heard*, in which he relates his experiences in preaching the gospel. We were deeply touched in reading this book. Though just an ordinary brother, neither highly educated nor especially gifted, he offered himself wholly to the Lord and was mightily used by Him. One thing characterized him: He was a broken man; his spirit was pure. While in a meeting listening to a preacher, he was so burdened for souls that he asked the preacher for permission to speak. He went to the pulpit, but no words came. His inner man so burned with a passion for souls that his tears gushed forth in torrents. In all, he managed to utter just a few incoherent sentences. Yet God's Spirit filled that meeting place; people were convicted of their sins and their lost estate. Here was a young man who was broken—he had few words, but when his spirit came forth people were mightily moved. In reading his autobiography we recognize that here was one whose spirit was wholly released. He was the instrument for saving many in his lifetime.

This is the way to preach the gospel. Whenever you see someone who is unsaved, you sense you should give him the gospel. You must allow your spirit to be released. To preach the gospel is purely a matter of having the outward man broken so that the inward man can flow forth and touch others. When your spirit touches another's spirit, God's Spirit quickens that spirit which is in darkness so that one may be wonderfully saved. However, if your spirit is bound by the outward man, God has no outlet in you and the gospel is blocked. This is why we focus so much attention on the dealing with the outward man. If we lack that dealing, we are powerless to win souls, though we may have all the doctrines memorized. Salvation comes when our spirit touches another's spirit. Then that soul cannot but prostrate himself at God's feet. Oh Beloved, when our spirit is truly released, souls will surely be saved.

Once people are saved, God does not want them to wait before dealing with sins, to wait more years before consecration, and to wait still longer before answering the call to really follow the Lord. As soon as people believe, they should immediately turn from their sins, wholly consecrate themselves to the Lord, and break the power of mammon. Their story should be like those recorded in the Gospels and in the Acts. For the gospel to have its fullest effect in man, the Lord must have a way in the lives of the messengers of the gospel.

In these years we have been wholly convinced the Lord is working toward recovery. The gospel of grace and the gospel of the kingdom must be joined together. In the Gospels, these two are never separated. Only in later years does it seem that those who have heard the gospel of grace know little or nothing of the gospel of the kingdom. Thus the two have been separated. But the time now is ripe for them to be united, so that people are thoroughly saved, forsaking everything and wholly consecrating themselves to the Lord.

Let us bow our heads before the Lord and acknowledge that the gospel must be fully preached and its messengers be fully dealt with. For the gospel to enter into men we must allow God to be manifested through us. As the effective preaching of the gospel requires more power, so the messengers of the gospel must pay a higher price. We must put everything on the altar. Let us pray thus: "Lord, I put my all on the altar. Find a way through me that the church may also find in me a way. I would not be one who blocks Thee and blocks the church."

The Lord Jesus never restricted God in any way. For nearly two thousand years God has been working in the church towards the day when the church will no longer restrict Him. As Christ fully manifests God, so shall it be with the church. Step by step God is instructing and dealing with His children; again and again we sense His hand upon us. So shall it be until that day when the church is indeed the full manifestation of God. Today let us turn to the Lord and confess: "Lord, we are ashamed. We have delayed Thy work; we have hindered Thy life; we have blocked the spread of the gospel; and we have limited Thy power." Individually in our hearts let us commit ourselves to Him afresh, saying: "Lord, I put my all on the altar, that Thou mayest get a way in me."

If we expect the effectiveness of the gospel to be fully recovered, consecration must be thorough. We must consecrate ourselves to God even like those in the early church. May God have an outlet through us.

Brokenness

and Discipline

FOR THE OUTWARD MAN to be broken, a full consecration is imperative. Yet we must understand that this crisis act alone will not solve our whole problem in service. Consecration is merely an expression of our willingness to be in the hands of God, and it can take place in just a few minutes. Do not think God can *Finish* His dealings with us in this short time. Though we are willing to offer outselves completely to God, we are just starting on the spiritual road. It is like entering the gate. After consecration, there must be the discipline of the Holy Spirit—this is the pathway. It takes consecration plus the discipline of the Holy Spirit to make us vessels fit for the Master's use. Without consecration, the Holy Spirit encounters difficulty in disciplining us. Yet consecration cannot serve as a substitute for His discipline.

Here then is a vital distinction: our consecration can only be according to the measure of our spiritual insight and understanding, but the Holy Spirit disciplines according to His own light. We really do not know how much our consecration involves. Our light is so limited that when it seems to us to be at its greatest, in God's view it is like pitch blackness. God's requirement so far exceeds what we can possibly consecrate — that is, in our limited light. The discipline of the Holy Spirit, on the other hand, is meted out to us according to our need as seen in God's own light. He knows our special need, and so by His Spirit He orders our circumstances in such a way as to bring about the breaking of the outward man. Notice how far the discipline of the Holy Spirit transcends our consecration.

Since the Holy Spirit works according to the light of God, His discipline is thorough and complete. We often wonder at the things which befall us, yet if left to ourselves we may be mistaken in our very best choice. The discipline He orders transcends our understanding. How often we are caught unprepared and conclude that surely such a drastic thing is not our need. Many times His discipline descends upon us suddenly without our having prior notice! We may insist we are living in "the light" but the Holy Spirit is dealing with us according to God's light. From the time we received Him, He has been ordering our circumstances for our profit according to His knowledge of us.

The working of the Holy Spirit in our lives has its positive as well as its negative side—that is to say, there is both a constructive and a destructive phase. After we are born again the Holy Spirit dwells in us, but our outward man so often deprives Him of His freedom. It is like trying to walk in a pair of ill-fitting new shoes. Because our outward and inward man are at variance with each other, God must employ whatever means He thinks effective in breaking down any stronghold over which our inward man has no control.

It is not by the supply of grace to the inward man that the Holy Spirit breaks the outward. Of course, God wants the inward man to be strong, but His method is to utilize external means to decrease our outward man. It would be well nigh impossible for the inward man to accomplish this, since these two are so different in nature that they can scarcely inflict any wound on each other. The nature of the outward man and that of external things are similar; and thus the former can be easily affected by the latter. External things can strike the outward man most painfully. So it is that God uses external things in dealing with our outward man.

You remember the Bible says that two sparrows are sold for a farthing (Matt. 10:29) and that five sparrows are sold for two farthings (Lk. 12:6). This is certainly cheap, and the fifth sparrow is included free. However, "one of them shall not fall to the ground without your Father; but of you even the hairs of the head are all numbered" (Matt. 10:29, 30). Not only is every hair counted, but every single one is also numbered. Hence we may be sure that all our circumstances are ordered by God. Nothing is accidental.

God's ordering is according to His knowledge of our needs, and with a view to the shattering of our outward man. Knowing that a certain external thing will thus affect us, He arranges for us to encounter it once, twice, and perhaps even more. Do you not realize that all the events of your life for the past five or ten years were ordered by God for your education? If you murmured and complained, you grievously failed to recognize His hand. If you thought you were just unfortunate, you were in ignorance of the discipline of the Holy Spirit. Remember that whatever happens to us is measured by the hand of God for our supreme good. Though probably it is not what we would choose, God knows what is best for us. Where would we be today had God not so disciplined us through ordering our circumstances? It is this very thing which keeps us pure and walking in His pathway. How foolish are those who have murmurings in their mouths and rebellion in their hearts at the very things the Holy Spirit has measured to them for their good.

As soon as we are saved, the Holy Spirit begins to deal out discipline; but He cannot act freely until our consecration is complete. After one is saved but not yet consecrated, and while he still loves himself much more than the Lord, the Holy Spirit is nonetheless working to bring him under control and break down his outward man that He may work unhinderedly.

Finally, there comes a time when you realize that you cannot live *by* yourself and *for* yourself. In the dim light you have, you come to God and say: "I consecrate myself to Thee. Come life or death, I have committed myself into Thy hands." This will strengthen the work of the Holy Spirit in your life. Herein lies the importance of consecration: it allows the Holy Spirit to work without restriction. So think it not strange when many unexpected things befall you after your consecration.

You have told the Lord: "Lord! Do whatever Thou deemest best in my life." Now that you have thus put yourself unconditionally in His hands, the Holy Spirit can freely work in you. To wholeheartedly decide to follow the Lord, you must pay close attention to the disciplinary work of the Holy Spirit.

The Greatest Means of Grace

God has been bestowing His grace upon us from the day we were saved. The ways by which we may receive grace from God are called the "means of grace." Prayer and listening to a message are two examples, for through them we can draw near to God and receive grace. This descriptive term, "the means of grace," has been universally accepted by the Church down through the centuries. We receive grace through meetings, through messages, through prayers, and so forth. But surely the greatest means of grace which we cannot afford to neglect is the discipline of the Holy Spirit. Nothing can be compared with this means of grace—not prayer, Bible readings, meetings, messages, meditation, or praise. Among all the God-given means of grace, it would seem this is the most important.

Tracing this means of grace can show us how far we have gone with the Lord. What we experience daily, at home or school or factory or on the road, is ordered by the Holy Spirit for our highest benefit. If we are not profited by this greatest means of grace, we suffer terrible loss. None of the other means can replace it, precious though they all are. Messages feed us, prayer restores us, God's word refreshes us, and helping others releases our spirit. But should our outward man remain strong, we give all who contact us the impression of being mixed and impure. People will recognize our zeal but also our mixed motives, our love toward the Lord but also our love for ourself. They feel we are a precious brother, yet a difficult one, for our outward man has not been broken. Let us not forget that though we are built up through messages, prayer, and the Bible, the greatest means of edification is the discipline of the Holy Spirit.

Henceforth there must be on our part a complete consecration so that we submit to what the Holy Spirit orders. Such submission brings blessing to us. If, instead , we quarrel with God and follow our own inclinations, we shall miss the way of His blessing. Once we realize that all of God's orderings are for our highest profit—even things troublesome to us — and are willing to accept these as disciplinary measures from Him, we shall see how the Holy Spirit will make use of all things in dealing with us.

Dealings of Various Kinds

Whatever the things to which you are bound, God will deal with them one after another. Not even such trivialities as clothing, eating or drinking can escape the careful hand of the Holy Spirit. He will not neglect one area in your life. You may even be ignorant of your affinity for a certain thing, but He knows and will deal with it most thoroughly. Until the day comes when all these things are destroyed, you do not know perfect liberty. In these dealings you can finally recognize the thoroughness of the Holy Spirit. Things long forgotten are brought to mind by the Lord. God's works are perfect, and nothing less than perfection can satisfy Him. He cannot stop short. Sometimes He will deal with you through others, arranging for you to be with someone whom you are angry with, or whom you despise or are jealous of; or very often it is through those you love. Before this you did not know how unclean and mixed you were, but afterwards you realize how much "rubbish" there is in you. You thought you were wholly for the Lord, but after receiving the discipline of the Holy Spirit you begin to see how far-reaching are the effects external things have upon you.

Then again the hand of God may touch our thought life. We discover that our thoughts are confused, independent, uncontrolled. We feign to be wiser than others. Then it is that the Lord allows us to crash into a wall and hit the dust—all to show us that we dare not use our thoughts inordinately. Once we have been enlightened in this, we shall fear our own thoughts as fire. Just as a hand withdraws immediately from a flame, so we shall instantly draw back when we encounter our uncontrolled thoughts. We shall remind ourselves, "This is not what I should think; I am afraid to pursue my own thoughts."

Further, God will so arrange our circumstances as to deal with our emotions. Some people are extremely emotional. When they are elated, they cannot contain themselves; when they are depressed, they cannot be comforted. Their whole life revolves around their emotions, with their elation resulting in dissipation and their depression in inactivity. How does God rectify this? He places them in situations where they dare not be too happy when elated, nor too sad when depressed. They can only depend upon the grace of God and live by His mercy, not by their fickle emotions.

Although difficulties with thoughts and emotions are quite common, the greatest and most prevalent difficulty is with the will. Our emotions run wild because our wills have not been dealt with. The root is in our will. The same is true with our thoughts. We may be able to mouth the word, "Not my will but Thine be done," but how often do we really allow the Lord to take over when things happen? The less you know yourself, the more easily you utter such words. The less you are enlightened, the easier submission to God seems to be. He who speaks cheaply has proved he has never paid the price.

Only after being dealt with by God do we really see how hard we are and how ready we are to have our own opinion. God must deal with us to make our wills tender and docile. Strong-willed people are convinced their feelings, ways and judgments are always right. Consider how Paul received this grace recorded in Philippians : "Do not trust in flesh" (3:3). We must also be led by God to such a place that we dare not trust our own judgment. God will allow us to make mistake after mistake until we realize that this will be our pattern for the future too. We truly need the grace of the Lord. Frequently the Lord permits us to reap serious consequences from our own judgments.

Finally, you will be so stricken by your failures that you will say: "I fear my own judgment as I fear hell fire. Lord, I am prone to mistakes. Unless Thou art merciful to me, unless Thou dost support me, unless Thou dost restrain me with Thy hand, I will be wrong again." This is the beginning of the destruction of the outward man: when you dare no longer to trust yourself. Your opinions usually come easily until you have been dealt with repeatedly by God and have suffered many failures. Then you yield and say: "God, I dare not think, I dare not decide." This is the discipline of the Holy Spirit: when all kinds of things and all sorts of people are pressing in from all directions.

Do not think there will be any slackening of this lesson! Very often the supply of God's word may be lacking or another means of grace may be insufficient, yet this special means of grace—the discipline of the Holy Spirit—is ever with us. You may say you have no opportunity to hear and be supplied by His word, yet this can never be true of the discipline of the Holy Spirit. Daily He is arranging ample opportunities for you to learn.

Once you yield yourself to God, this discipline will meet

your need to a far greater extent than will the supply of His word. It is not just for the learned, the clever, the gifted; no, it is the way for every child of God. The supply of God's word, the power of prayer, the fellowship of the believers— none of these can substitute for the discipline of the Holy Spirit. This is because you need not only to be built up; you need also to be broken, to be delivered of all the many things in your life that cannot be brought over into eternity.

The Cross in Operation

The cross is more than a doctrine; it must be put into practice. Do not think that the way to humility is to be constantly reminding ourselves not to be proud. We must be stricken again and again — even if it means twenty times— until we surrender and are proud no more. Let us never assume this comes about merely by following the teaching of a certain brother. No, it is because our pride has been broken through God's dealing.

Through the operation of the cross we shall learn to depend upon the grace of God, not on our memory. Whether we remember or not, the fact remains, He is accomplishing a work which is dependable and lasting. Formerly, the outward and the inward man were not able to join hands; but now the outward man waits meekly, in fear and trembling, before God.

Everyone of us is in need of this discipline from the Lord. As we review our past history, we cannot but see the hand of God in dealing with the independence, pride, and selfishness of our outward man. We discover the meaning of the things that have happened to us.

Dividing

and Revelation

GOD DESIRES not only to break down the outward man, but also to separate it so that the inward man may no longer be entangled in the outward man's activities. Or, we may simply say, God wants to divide our spirit and soul.

How rare it is these days to find a pure spirit. Usually whenever our spirit comes forth, so does our soul; they are mixed. So the first requirement in God's work is a pure, not a powerful spirit. Those who neglect this, though their work may be done in power, will find it destroyed due to the lack of purity. Though they may truly posess the power of God, yet because their spirit is mixed, they are destroying what they build. Let us see if we can understand how this is.

Some may think that as long as they receive power from God, all their natural abilities will be owned of Him. Not so! The more we know God, the more we know and love a pure spirit — a purity which allows no mingling of the outward with the inward. One whose outward man has not been dealt with cannot expect the power that flows from within him to be pure. For spiritual power to be mixed as it comes from oneself, even if the results seem good, constitutes a sin before God.

Many young brothers, knowing well that the gospel is the power of God, still insinuate their own cleverness, their jests, and their personal feelings into their preaching of the gospel; thus people touch them as well as God's power. Though they themselves may not sense it, others who are pure in spirit will instantly detect such impurities. How often our zeal in labor is mixed with natural pleasure. We are doing the will of God because it happens to coincide with ours. In standing firm for God we are merely expressing our strong personality.

Since our greatest problem is this impurity, God must so work in our lives that our outward man is broken and we are refined of our impurities. While God is breaking our hard outer shell, He is also doing the work of refining. Thus we see His two-fold dealings with us: *breaking down the outward man,* and *dividing it from the spirit.* The first is done through the discipline of the Holy Spirit, while the latter is through the Spirit's revelation.

The Need to Be Broken and Divided

The outward man needs to be broken for the spirit to be released. But when the spirit comes forth, it must not be clouded by the outward man. This problem takes us further than the release of the spirit, for it touches upon the spirit's cleanliness or purity.

If one is not enlightened as to the nature of the outward man, and is thus not strictly judged before God, his outward man will automatically come out together with his spirit. While he is ministering before God, we can tell that he himself has also come out. He may exhibit God, but he also exhibits his unjudged self. Is it not strange that our most prominent part, our strongest point, always touches others? Our unjudged outward man will project his strongest point on others. This is beyond pretension. How can you expect to become spiritual in the pulpit if you are not spiritual in your room? Can you project yourself into spirituality? However hard you may try, you stand revealed whenever you open your mouth. If you truly desire to be delivered, God must deal with your strong point in a basic way, not just superficially. Only after He has broken you in this can your spirit be released without impurities being inflicted upon others.

Impurity is the biggest problem in the lives of God's servants. Frequently we touch both life and death in our brother. We find God but also self, a meek spirit but also stubbornness, the Holy Spirit but also the flesh — all in the same person. When he stands up to speak, he impresses others with a mixed spirit, a spirit which is not clean. Thus, for God to use you as a minister of His word, for you to be His mouthpiece, you must seek His favor by praying: "O God, do a work in me, to break, to divide, my outward man." Otherwise, the Lord's Name will suffer loss. You are giving to men that which is of yourself while ministering God's word. The Lord's Name does not suffer because of your lack of life, but because of your flow of impurities. The church likewise suffers.

Now that we have considered the discipline of the Holy Spirit, what about the revelation of the Holy Spirit? The discipline of the Spirit may precede His revelation, or may follow. There is no fixed order; with some He may begin with His discipline, in others with His revelation. However, it is certain that the discipline of the Holy Spirit exceeds His revelation. We are referring of course to the experience of God's children, and not to doctrine. To most, it will seem that discipline plays a much larger part than revelation.

How the Living Word Divides

"For the word of God is living and operative, and sharper than any two-edged sword, and penetrating to the division of soul and spirit, both of joints and marrow, and a discerner of the thoughts and intents of the heart. And there is not a creature unapparent before him; but all things are naked and laid bare to his eyes, with whom we have to do" (Heb. 4:12,13).

The first thing to be noticed is that the word of God is living. His word is sure to be living when we see it. For if we do not find it living, we simply have failed to see God's word. We may have read over the words of the Bible, but if we do not touch something living, we do not see God's word.

John 3:16 says: "For God so loved the world, that he gave his only begotten Son, that whosoever believes on him may not perish, but have life eternal." Consider how one hears such a word; he kneels down and prays: "Lord, I thank Thee and praise Thee, for Thou hast loved me and saved me!" We immediately know this man has touched the word of God, for His word has become living to him. Another man may sit by his side, listening to the very same words but not actually hear the word of God. There is no living response from him. We can draw but one conclusion: since God's word is living, he who listens and does not live has not heard the word of God.

Not only is the word of God living; it is also operative. "Living" points to its nature, while "operative" applies to its ability to fulfill the work on man. God's word cannot return void; it will prevail and accomplish its purpose. It is not mere word, but word that will so operate as to produce results.

What then does God's word do for us? It penetrates and divides. It is sharper than any two-edged sword. Its sharpness is demonstrated in the "penetrating to the division of soul and spirit, both of joints and marrow." Note the analogy here: the two-edged sword against joints and marrow, and the word of God against soul and spirit. Joints and marrow are embedded deeply in the human body. To separate the joints is to cut across the bones; to divide the marrow is to crack the bones. Only two things are harder to be divided than the joints and marrow: the soul and spirit. No sword, however sharp, can divide them. Similarly, we are wholly unable to distinguish between what is soul and what is spirit. Yet the Scripture tells us how the living word of God can do the job, for it is sharper than any two-edged sword. God's word is living, operative, and able to penetrate and divide. It is the soul and spirit of man which are thus penetrated and divided. Perhaps someone may raise this question: "It doesn't seem that the word of God has done anything special in me. I have often heard God's words and even received revelation, but I do not know what penetrating is, nor do I understand this dividing. As far as I can tell, I am a stranger to both these processes."

How does the Bible answer this question for us? It says "penetrating to the division of soul and spirit, both of joints and marrow," but it also goes on to say that it is "a discerner of the thoughts and intents of the heart." "Thoughts" refers to what we deliberate in our heart and "intents" has reference to our motives. Thus the word of God is able to discern both what we think and what motivates the thinking.

Too often we can easily identify what comes from the outward man. We quite glibly confess, "This was soulish, for it came from self." But we do not really "see" what the soul or self is. Then one day God's mercy comes to us, His light shines upon us and His voice announces to us with severity and solemnity: "What you frequently refer to as your self *is* your self! You have talked lightly and easily about the flesh. You must 'see' how God hates this and will not allow such to continue."

Before this "seeing" we have been able to talk jokingly about the flesh; but once we are stricken with light we shall confess: "Ah, this is it! This is what I have talked about." Thus we have more than an intellectual dividing. It is the word of God that comes upon us to point out to us what we conceive and purpose in our heart. We receive a two-fold enlightenment: how our thoughts originate from the flesh, and how our intentions are entirely selfish.

To illustrate this let us consider two unconverted persons. One is aware that he is a sinner. He has been to many meetings and heard many messages on sin. Clear preaching has brought him to acknowledge himself as a sinner. Yet when he thus refers to himself, he can mention it laughingly, as if it does not really matter. Another hears the same messages, and the light of God shines upon him. The Spirit so convicts him that he prostrates himself on the ground and prays: "Oh, this is what I am — a sinner!" Not only has he heard by the word of God that he is a sinner, he has also "seen" that this is his true condition. He condemns himself. He is stricken to the ground. Thus enlightened, he can confess his sin and receive the salvation of the Lord. He will henceforth never speak lightly or jokingly of the sin he has "seen." But the first one, who can jokingly describe himself as a sinner, has not "seen" and hence is not saved.

How do you react to this message today that your outward man seriously interferes with God and must be broken by Him? If you can begin talking about it freely and easily, it surely has not touched you. If, on the other hand, you are enlightened by it, you will say, "O Lord, today I begin to know myself. Until now I have not recognized my outward man." And as the light of God surrounds you, uncovering your outward man, you fall to the ground, no longer able to stand. Instantly you "see" what you are.

Once you said you loved the Lord, but under God's light you find it is not so — you really love yourself. This light really divides you and sets you apart. You are inwardly separated, not by your mentality, nor by mere teaching, but by God's light. Once you said you were zealous for the Lord, but now the light of God shows you that your zeal was entirely stirred by your own flesh and blood. You thought you loved sinners while preaching the gospel, but now the light has come, and you discover that your preaching the gospel stems mainly from your love of action, your delight in speaking, your natural inclination. The deeper this divine light shines, the more the intent and thought of your heart is revealed. Once you assumed that your thoughts and intents were of the Lord, but in this piercing light you know they are entirely of yourself. Such light brings you down before God.

Too often what we supposed was of the Lord proves to be

of ourselves. Though we had proclaimed that our messages were given by the Lord, now the light of heaven compels us to confess that the Lord has not spoken to us, or, if He has, how little He has said. How much of the Lord's work, so-called, turns out to be carnal activities! This unveiling of the real nature of things enlightens us to the true knowledge of what is of *ourselves* and what is of the *Lord,* how much is *from the soul* and how much is *from the spirit.* How wonderful if we can announce: His light has shone; our spirit and soul are divided, and the thoughts and intents of our heart are discerned.

You who have experienced this know it is beyond mere teaching. All efforts to distinguish what is of self and what is of the Lord, to separate what things are of the outward man from what are of the inward man — even to the extent of listing them item by item and then memorizing them — have proved to be so much wasted effort. You continue to behave just as usual, for you cannot get rid of your outward man. You may be able to condemn the flesh, you may be proud that you can identify such and such as belonging to the flesh, but you still are not delivered from it.

Deliverance comes from the light of God. When that light shines, you immediately see how superficial and fleshly has been your denial of the flesh, how natural has been your criticism of the natural. But now the Lord has laid bare to your eyes the thoughts and intents of your heart. You fall prostrate before Him and say: "O Lord! Now I know these things are really from my outward man. Only this light can really divide my outward from my inner."

So it is that even our denial of the outward man, and our determination to reject it, will not help. Yes, even the very confession of our sin is for naught, and our tears of repentance need to be washed in the blood. How foolish to imagine that we could expose our sin! Only in His Light shall we "see" and be exposed. It must be His work by the Spirit, not our efforts of the soul—that is, not out of our own mind. This is God's only way.

This is why God says, "My word is living and effectual. My sword is the sharpest of all. When My word comes to man it is able to divide the soul and spirit, just as a two-edged sword can divide the joints and marrow."

How does it divide? By revealing the thought and intent of our heart. We do not know our own heart. Beloved, only those who are in the light know their own heart. No one else does, not one! Yet when God's word comes, we "see." We are exposed as self-centered, seeking only gratification, glory, pre-eminence and prestige for self. How blessed is that light which causes us to fall down at His feet.

What Is a Revelation?

The Scripture we have been considering continues thus: "And there is not a creature unapparent before him; but all things are naked and laid bare to his eyes, with whom we have to do." Here the Lord gives us the standard or criterion for dividing. What constitutes a revelation by the Holy Spirit? How much must we see before it is a revelation? Heb. 4:13 can help us answer this. *Revelation enables us to see what God sees.* All things are naked and laid bare before Him. Any covering is upon our own eyes, not God's. When God opens our eyes that we may know the intent of our heart and the deepest thought within us in the measure that He Himself knows us — this is revelation. As we are naked and laid bare before Him, so are we before ourselves as we receive revelation. This is revelation: for us to be allowed to see what our Lord sees.

Should God be merciful to us and grant us even a small measure of revelation, so that we can see ourselves as we are seen by Him, we shall immediately be smitten to the ground. We need not try to be humble. Those who live in the light cannot be proud. It is only while dwelling in darkness that we can be proud. Outside of God's light men can be arrogant and haughty; but under the revelation of the light they can only prostrate themselves before Him.

As you proceed it becomes more evident that it is extremely difficult to explain this matter of dividing the natural from the spiritual, the outward from the inward. Only as there is revelation is the problem solved. Whenever you are enabled to discern the thoughts and intents of your heart, you can be sure your soul and spirit are being divided.

If you desire to be used by God, sooner or later you will let the light shine upon you. You will turn to Him and say: "O God, I am absolutely unreliable. I do not know whom I am accusing, nor what sin I am confessing. Only in Thy light am I able to know." Before you receive enlightenment you may say you are a sinner, but you lack a sinner's contrition; you may think you hate yourself, but you have no real sense of self-abhorrence; you may say you deny yourself, but the feeling of abnegation is missing. Once the light comes, the surface covering is pulled away and the "real" or "original" is revealed. What an unveiling to see I only love myself; to see I am deceived, and cheating the Lord; to see I do not love Him. This light shows you what you are and what you have been doing. Henceforth you will have the inner knowledge of what belongs to self. Without this judgment by the light, you cannot even imitate, but now as the light of God judges, spirit and soul are divided; imitation is impossible.

What the Lord does is to pierce into our inner man with a penetrating light. It may happen while we are listening to a message, or praying by ourselves, or fellowshipping with others, or even walking alone. This incomparable light shows us how much belongs to ourselves. It reveals to us that scarcely anything that proceeds from ourselves is from the Lord. In conversation, in activities, in works, in zeal, in preaching, in helping others — in every field of life how all-pervading is our self. Yet once our hidden self is brought to light, our condemnation of the outward man will be spontaneous. On subsequent occasions, whenever it expresses itself we will instantly regret it and judge it. It is only after such enlightenment that we are able to divide the spirit and soul. We will henceforth live before the Lord with our spirit released. It is pure now, and offers no difficulty to the Lord.

Thus the dividing of spirit and soul depends upon enlightenment; that is, we are able to see as God sees. Just what does God see? He sees what we do not see. We are blind to what is of ourselves, thinking it is of God while actually it is not. What we professed to be good, by that light we now condemn. What we considered as right, we now reject. What passed for spiritual we now recognize as soulish. And what we thought was of God we now know to be of self. We confess: "Lord! Now I come to know myself. I have been blind for twenty or thirty years, and I did not realize it. I have not seen as Thou hast seen."

Such a seeing delivers you from the dead weight of self. Seeing is His dealing. The word of God is effective, for it enlightens you to the casting off of the outward man. It is not that after you have heard the word of God you gradually change yourself, as if seeing is one step and casting off another. No, enlightenment is itself a casting off; the two occur simultaneously. As soon as the light strikes, the flesh is dead. No flesh can live in that light. The moment one comes into the light he prostrates himself. The light has dried up his flesh. Beloved, this is effectiveness. Indeed the word of God is living and operative. God does not speak and then wait for you to produce. His word is effective in your life.

May the Lord open our eyes to see the importance of the discipline of the Holy Spirit and His revelation. These two join hands in dealing effectively with our outward man. Let us look to God for His grace to enable us to place ourselves under His light and to be so enlightened as to bow before Him, acknowledging: "Lord, how foolish and blind I have been all these years in mistaking what flows from me as coming from Thee. Lord, be merciful to me!"

What Impression

Do We Give?

WHETHER WE CAN do the Lord's work depends not so much on *our words or actions*, but rather on what *comes forth* from us. We are not able to edify others if we say one thing and emit from our lives another thing, if we act one way and live another way. What emanates from us is an important consideration.

We often say that our impression of a certain person is good or bad. How do we receive such an impression? It is not just from his words, nor even from his actions. A mysterious something expresses itself while he is speaking or acting. It is this which gives us the impression.

What others sense in us is our most outstanding feature. If our mind has never been dealt with and is undisciplined, naturally we shall use our mind to contact people, and they will be struck by its forcefulness. Or if we possess an inordinate affection, if we are overly warm or cold, others will take note of this in their impression of us. Whatever our strongest characteristic is, it invariably will stand out and impress others. We may be able to control our speech or action, but we are unable to restrain that which expresses our nature. What we are, we cannot but reveal.

II Kings 4 recounts how the Shunammite received Elisha. "And it came to pass on a day that Elisha passed to Shunem, where was a wealthy woman, and she constrained him to eat bread. And so it was, that as oft as he passed by, he turned in thither to eat bread. And she said to her husband, Behold now, I perceive that this is a holy man of God, who passes by us continually." Note that Elisha preached no sermon, worked no miracle. He merely dropped in and ate whenever he was passing that way. By the way he ate, the woman recognized him as a holy man of God. This was the impression Elisha gave to others.

We should ask ourselves, what impression do I give to others? How often we have emphasized the need for our outward man to be broken. If this brokenness is not accomplished, others meet the impact of our outward man. Whenever we are in their presence they are made uncomfortable by our self-love, or pride, or obstinacy, or cleverness, or eloquence. Perhaps the impression we leave is a favorable one, but is God being satisfied? Will such an impression meet the church's need? If God is not satisfied, and the church is not helped, any impression we leave is for naught.

Beloved, God's full intention requires that our spirit be released. It is imperative for the growth of the church. How urgent, then, that our outward man be broken! Without this breaking our spirit cannot come forth, and the impression we leave with others will not be a spiritual one.

Suppose a brother is speaking on the Holy Spirit. Though his subject is the Holy Spirit, his words, his attitudes, and his illustrations are full of himself. Perhaps without knowing why, the audience inwardly suffers while listening to him. His mouth is full of the Holy Spirit, yet the impression he leaves with his listeners is of himself. What is the spiritual value of such empty talk? None.

Rather than stressing teaching, let us place more emphasis

on what it is that comes forth from us. God is not watching to see if our teaching becomes deeper; He wants to lay hold of us as individuals. If our nature is not properly dealt with, we may give forth so-called spiritual teaching, but there is no spiritual impartation. How tragic when we merely impress the outward man yet do not impart something of a life impression to the inward man!

Again and again God arranges our circumstances to break us in our strong point. You may be stricken once, twice, but still the third blow must come. God will not let you go. He will not stay His hand until He has broken that prominent feature in you.

What the Holy Spirit accomplishes when we are being disciplined is totally different from what happens when we are hearing a message. A message we hear may often remain in our mind for several months, possibly even years, before its truth will become operative in us. Thus the hearing often precedes the real entering into life. However, through the disciplining of the Holy Spirit, we more quickly see the truth and thus possess it. How strange that we grasp mere knowledge through a message much faster than we learn reality through discipline! Once we hear, we remember. But we may be disciplined ten times and still wonder why. The day discipline accomplishes its purpose is the day you really "see" the truth and enter into its reality. So the work of the Holy Spirit is to break you down on the one hand and to build you up on the other. Thus your heart will say: "Thanks be unto the Lord. Now I know that His disciplining hand upon me for these past five or ten years has been just to break this strong point in me."

The Amazing Work of Slaying through Enlightenment

Having considered the disciplinary working of the Holy Spirit, now let us see how He employs another means to deal with our outward man. Besides discipline there will be enlightenment. Sometimes these two are used simultaneously, sometimes alternately. At times the discipline is shown in circumstances aimed at leveling our outstanding feature: at other times God graciously shines upon us to enlighten us. The flesh, as we know, lives hidden in darkness. Many works of the flesh are allowed to exist because they are not recognized by us as such. Once His light reveals the flesh to us we tremble, not daring to move.

We have especially observed this at times when the church is rich in the word of God. When the ministry of His word is strong and there is no lack of prophetic ministry, light breaks out clear and strong. In such light you come to realize that even your condemnation of your pride is itself pride. In fact, your very talking against your pride is boastful. Thus, as soon as you see pride in the light you are sure to say, "Alas! So this is pride — how abhorrent and unclean it is!" Pride seen in the light of revelation differs completely from the pride talked about so glibly. Enlightenment exposes the true condition. Immediately it dawns upon you that you are ten thousand times worse than any of your preconceived notions of yourself. Right then your pride, your self, your flesh wither away and die with no hope of survival.

Whatever is revealed "in the light" is slain by it. This is most marvelous. We are not first enlightened and then, with the passage of time, gradually brought into death. Rather we fall down instantaneously at the coming of light. As the Holy Spirit reveals, we are dealt with. Revelation, then, includes both seeing and slaying. It is God's unique way of dealing. Once the uncleanness is really exposed, it cannot remain. Therefore light both reveals and slays.

This being slain by the light is one of the most needful Christian experiences. Paul did not rush to the roadside and kneel down when the light shone upon him. He fell to the ground. Though naturally capable and self-confident, he reacted to the light by falling down somewhat perplexed, yet inwardly exposed. How effectual was this light which struck him to the ground! Let us note that this happened all at once. We might assume that God first enlightens our understanding and then leaves us to work it out. That is not God's way.

God always shows us how hateful and polluted we are, and our immediate response is: "Alas! What a wretch I am — so unclean, so despicable!" For God to reveal our true self is to fall down as dead. Once a proud person has been truly enlightened, he cannot so much as make an attempt to be proud anymore. The effect of that enlightenment will have its mark upon him all his days.

On the other hand, this time of enlightenment is also the time for believing — not for asking, but for bowing low. God follows the same principle in saving us as He does in working in us afterwards. When the radiancy of the gospel shines upon us, we do not pray: "Lord, I beseech Thee to be my Savior." To pray thus, even for days, would bring no assurance of salvation. We simply say: "Lord, I receive Thee as my Savior." Instantly salvation happens! In like manner, in God's subsequent working, as soon as light comes upon us we should immediately prostrate ourselves under His light and tell the Lord: "Lord, I accept Thy sentence. I agree with Thy judgment." This will prepare us for more light.

In that hour of unveiling, even noble deeds — performed in His name and in love to Him — will somehow lose their luster. In every highest purpose you will detect the meanest inclination. What you considered as wholly for God now appears to be riddled with self. Alas! Self seems to permeate every vestige of your being, robbing God of glory.

To us it has seemed there is no depth which man himself cannot plumb! Yet it takes God's revelation to expose man's real condition. God will not stop until He lays us bare that we may see ourselves. At first He alone knows us, for we are always bare and naked before Him. But once God has disclosed to us the thoughts and intents of our heart, we are then laid bare before ourselves. How shall we ever lift up our head again? Leniency with ourselves becomes a thing of the past. Though we used to think we were better than others, now we know what we really are, and we are ashamed to show ourselves. We search in vain for a word adequate to describe our uncleanness and despicableness. Our shame weighs upon us, as though we bore the shame of the whole

world. Like Job we fall before the Lord and repent of ourselves: "I abhor myself and repent in dust and ashes. Surely I
am beyond healing."

Such enlightenment, such self-abhorrence, such shame
and humiliation, such repentance delivers us from the
bondage of long years. When the Lord enlightens, He delivers. Enlightenment is deliverance, and seeing is freedom.
Only thus does our flesh cease to operate, and our outward
shell is broken.

Discipline Compared with Revelation

Let us next compare the discipline and the revelation of
the Holy Spirit. The discipline of the Holy Spirit is usually a
slower process, repeated time and again perhaps for years
before the point at issue is finally dealt with. (Incidentally,
this discipline of the Holy Spirit oftentimes exists without
any supply of ministry.) Not so with the revelation of the
Holy Spirit. This often comes swiftly, within a few days or
possibly a few minutes. Under the light of God you will see in
a very little time your true condition and how useless you are.
Then too, revelation frequently comes through the supply of
God's word. That is why the revelation of the Holy Spirit
multiplies when the church is strong and the ministry of the
word of God is rich.

However, no one should imagine that in the absence of
such rich ministry and flowing revelation he is then free to
live according to his outward man. It is important to remember that the discipline of the Holy Spirit is still operative. Though one may be deprived of contact with other
believers for years, the presence of the Holy Spirit with him
is an assurance that he can arrive at a good spiritual state as
long as he is responsive to the Spirit's discipline. While the
weakness of the church may result in some members lacking
the supply of God's word, they have only themselves to
blame if they miss the value of the Spirit's discipline. Further,
their failure does not mean that the Holy Spirit has not or
does not discipline them. Rather, it means that the years of

discipline have produced no effect. Though the Lord has smitten once and again, they remained ignorant of its meaning. Like a stubborn horse or mule void of understanding, they seem not to fathom the Lord's mind—even after ten years of dealing. How pitiful are such! We can only make this conclusion: discipline is plentiful in many lives, but recognizing the hand of the Lord in that discipline is rare indeed.

How often when the Lord deals with us we see only the hand of man. This is entirely wrong. Like the Psalmist our attitude should be, "I was dumb, I opened not my mouth, for thou hast done it" (Psalm 39:9). We must remember that it is God who is dealing with us, not our brother or sister or any other person.

Has the Lord for years disciplined us, but instead of recognizing His hand we blamed it on other people or on fate? May we be reminded that *everything is measured by God for us.* He has predetermined its time, its boundary, and its force, in order to break our hard-to-deal-with outstanding feature. Oh, may we have the grace to recognize the meaning of His hand in seeking to shatter this outward man. Until that happens people will only meet that imperious self when they come in contact with us. Until that breaking is effected, our spirit cannot flow forth freely toward them.

Earnestly we pray that the church may know God as never before, that God's children may be increasingly fruitful unto Him. The Lord intends to bring us into the place where not only our gospel message and teaching ministry are correct but we as well are right. The issue is: can God be fully released through our spirit?

When the spirit is released, it supplies the needs of the world. No work is more important or thorough than this, and nothing can take its place. The Lord is not so much concerned with your teachings or sermons as He is with the impression you give. What is it that comes from you — that is the final yardstick? Do you impress people with yourself or with the Lord? Do you let people touch your teaching or your Lord? This is really vital, for it determines the value of all your labor and work.

Beloved, be assured the Lord pays far more attention to what comes out of your inner life than what comes out of your mouth. Do not forget that in every contact you make with another, something comes out of you. It is either yourself or God flowing forth, either your outward man or the spirit. Finally, I would ask, When you stand before people what is it that comes forth? And lest we are too quick to give an answer, let us remember that this basic question can only be rightly answered "in His light."

Meekness

in Brokenness

GOD'S METHOD in breaking our outward man varies according to the target. Let us explain the target this way: with some, it is their self-love; with others, their pride. Also there are those whose self-reliance and cleverness need to be destroyed; such will find themselves in one predicament after another, defeated at every turn until they learn to say, "We live not in fleshly wisdom but in God's grace." Moreover those whose outstanding feature is subjectivity will find themselves in circumstances peculiar to their need. And again, there are those who are always bubbling over with ideas and opinions. While the Bible affirms, "Is any matter too wonderful for Jehovah?", some brothers maintain that nothing is too hard for them! They boast they can do everything, yet strangely they fail in every undertaking. Things that seemed so easy fall apart in their hands. In perplexity they ask "Why?" This is the way the Holy Spirit deals with them to reach the necessary target. Such illustrations show how the target of the Spirit varies with the individual concerned.

There is also a variation in the tempo of the Holy Spirit's dealings. At times the blows may follow one upon another without respite; or there may be periods of lull. But all whom the Lord loves He scourges. Thus God's children bear wounds inflicted by the Holy Spirit. While the affliction may vary, the consequences are the same: the self within is wounded. So God touches our self-love or pride or cleverness or subjectivity, whichever constitutes His outward target. He intends by each blast at the target to further weaken us, until the day comes when we are crushed and pliable in His hands. Whether the dealing touches our affection or our thoughts, the final result is a producing of a broken will. We are all naturally obstinate. This stubborn will is supported by our thoughts, opinions, self-love, affection, or cleverness. This explains the variations in the Holy Spirit's dealings with us. In the final analysis God is after our will, for it is that which represents our self.

Thus a common feature marks out those who have been enlightened and disciplined—they become meek. Meekness is the sign of brokenness. All who are broken by God are characterized by meekness. Formerly we could afford to be obstinate because we were like a house well supported by many pillars. As God removes the pillars one after another, the house is bound to collapse. When the outside supports are demolished, self cannot but fall.

But we must learn to recognize true meekness. Do not be deceived into thinking that a soft-spoken voice indicates a gentle will. Often an iron will lies hidden behind the softest voice. Stubbornness is a matter of character, not of voice. Some who appear to be more gentle than others, are—before God—just as obstinate and selfish. For such there can only be the severity of His dealing until they dare not act presumptuously. God designs that seemingly outward dealings touch us to the core; never shall we be able to raise our heads in these particular matters. It is irrevocably settled that in these we cannot disobey the Lord; we dare not insist upon our opinion. Fear of the hand of the Lord restrains us. It is fear of God that makes us meek. The more we are broken through God's dealings, the meeker we become. To see true meekness is to behold inner brokenness.

Let us illustrate it this way: After contacting a certain brother, you may sense that he is truly gifted yet nonetheless find him to be unbroken. Many are like that—gifted but unbroken. Their unbrokenness can be easily detected. As soon as you meet them you sense an undertone in them— you can feel their obstinacy. Not so with one who is broken; there is a Spirit-wrought meekness. In whatever point one has been chastened by God, there he dare not boast. He has learned to fear God in this and is transformed into meekness. Please notice how the Scripture uses different metaphors to describe the Holy Spirit. He is like fire and like water. Fire speaks of His power, water of His cleansing. But in reference to His character He is said to be like a dove, meek and gentle. The Spirit of God will incorporate His nature in us little by little until we, too, are characterized by the dove. Meekness, born out of the fear of God, is the Holy Spirit's sign for brokenness.

Considering the Qualities of Meekness

One broken by the Spirit naturally possesses meekness. His contacts with people are no longer marked by that obstinacy, hardness, and sharpness which are the hallmarks of an unbroken man. He has been brought to the place where his attitude is as meek as his voice is gentle. The fear of God in his heart naturally finds expression in his words and manner.

(1) Approachable

There are several qualities which characterize a person who is meek. He is approachable—so easy to have contact with, to talk to, and to make inquiry of. He confesses his sin readily and sheds tears freely. How difficult it is for some to shed tears. It is not that there is any special value in tears, yet in one whose thought, will, and emotion have been dealt with by God, tears often denote his readiness to see and acknowledge his fault. He is easy to talk to, for his outward shell has been broken. Open to the opinions of others, he welcomes instructions and in this new position can be edified in all things.

(2) Highly Sensitive

Again, one who is meek is alert to his environment, since his spirit can easily come forth and touch the spirits within his brethren. The slightest movement in another's spirit does not go unnoticed by him. Almost immediately he can detect the true significance in a situation—whether it is right or wrong. Whatever the circumstance, his spirit readily responds. His actions are thoughful, nor will he inconsiderately hurt others' feelings.

Too often we persist in doing things which in others' spirits have already been condemned. Our outward man is not broken. Others sense it, but we do not. Consider how this may occur in prayer meetings, when the brothers and sisters may feel repugnance toward our prayers. Yet we drone on and on. Other brethren's spirits come forth and cry out, "Stop praying," but we remain insensitive. There is no response to the feelings of others. Not so with one whose outward man has been broken. Because the Spirit has wrought a deep sensitivity, he naturally touches, and can be touched, by the spirits of others. Such a one will not be dull to other's reactions.

(3) Ready for Corporate Life

Only these broken ones know what the body of Christ is. Without meekness they are hardly ready for participating in corporate life. They begin to touch the spirit of the body, even the feelings of other members. If one lacks this body-feeling he is like a false member of the body, like an artificial hand of Christ which may move with the physical body but has no feeling. The whole body has sensed it except him. Nor can he meekly receive instruction or correction. But a broken one can touch the conscience of the church and know the church's feeling, for his spirit is open to the spirit of the church to receive from it any communication.

How precious is this sensitivity! Whenever we do anything wrong, immediately we sense it. Though we are not freed from wrong-doing, we nevertheless possess a faculty which will quickly prick us. Brothers and sisters know you are wrong, but even before they open their mouth you are brought to your senses by mere contact with them. You have touched their spirit, and this indicates to you whether they approve or disapprove. It becomes evident that meekness, which is the fruit of brokenness, is a basic requirement, and without it body-life is impossible.

The body of Christ lives the same way as our physical body. It does not require the calling of a general council in order to reach decisions. Nor is there need for prolonged discussions; all the members naturally possess a common feeling and that feeling expresses the mind of the body. And what is more, it is also the expression of the mind of the Head. Thus the mind of the Head is known through that of the body. After our outward man is broken, we begin to live in that corporate awareness as related members of His body and are easily corrected.

(4) Easily Edified

The greatest advantage of brokenness, however, is not in having our wrong corrected but rather in enabling us to receive the supply of all the body. Our spirit is then released and open to get spiritual help from whatever source in the body. One who is not broken can hardly be helped. Suppose, for example, a brother has a keen but unbroken intellect. He may come to meetings, but he is untouched. Unless he meets one whose mind is sharper than his, he will not be helped. He will analyze the thoughts of the preacher and reject them as useless and meaningless. Months and years may thus pass by without his being touched. He is walled in by his mind and it would seem he can only be helped through it. In this condition he cannot receive spiritual edification. However, should the Lord come in and shatter this wall, showing him the futility of his own thoughts, he will become attentive as a child to what others may say. He will no longer despise people who seem to be below his capabilities or capacities.

In listening to a message he will use his spirit to contact the spirit of the preacher, rather than focusing upon the pronunciation of words or the presentation of doctrine. When the spirit of the preacher is released with a definite word from the Lord, his spirit is refreshed and edified. If one's spirit is free and open, he receives help whenever his brother's spirit comes forth. But remember, this is not the same as being helped doctrinally. The more a man's spirit has been dealt with by God the more thoroughly the outward man is broken and, accordingly, the greater help he can receive. And it is further true that whenever God's Spirit makes a move upon any brother, never again will he judge others merely by doctrine, words, or eloquence. His attitude is entirely changed. It is an invariable law: that the measure of anyone being helped depends upon the condition of his spirit.

Now we must clearly understand what is meant by being edified. It cannot mean expanded thoughts, nor improved understanding, nor greater doctrinal accumulation. It simply means that my spirit has once more contacted God's Spirit. It does not matter through whom the Spirit of God moves, whether in the meeting or in individual fellowship; I am none the less nourished and revived. My spirit is much like a mirror, which is polished every time.

Suppose we explain it like this: that whatever proceeds from the spirit brightens everything it touches. As individuals we are much like light bulbs—different colored light bulbs. Yet the color does not interfere with the passage of electricity through it. As soon as the electricity flows into it, it lights up. So is it in our spirit; when there is the flowing of His Spirit we will forget the theology we have learned. All we know is that the Spirit has come. Instead of mere knowledge we have an "inner light." We are revived and nourished in His presence.

Once our intellectuality made us impossible, but now we can easily be helped. Now we understand why it is hard for others to receive help. We understand that it requires spending much time in prayer before we can touch them in spirit. There is no other way to help an obstinate person. As we shall see in the next lesson there is a way God has designed for true effectiveness.

Two Very Different

Ways

WE MUST RECOGNIZE two very different ways of help before us. First, "there is a way that seemeth right" in which help is received from the outside—through the mind—by doctrine and its exposition. Many will even profess to have been greatly helped through this way. Yet it is a "help" so very different from that help which God really intends.

Second, we must see that God's way is the way of spirit touching spirit. Instead of having our mentality developed or acquiring a storehouse of knowledge, it is by this other means of contact that our spiritual life is built up. Let no one be deceived; until we have found this way we have not found true Christianity. This alone is the way of having our spirit edified or built up.

Let us explain it like this. If you are accustomed to sermons, no doubt it would annoy you to hear the same message from the same preacher twice. You feel sure it is enough to hear that message once. This is because your conception of

Christianity is simply doctrine—the storing of correct knowledge in your mind. Do you not realize that edification is not a question of doctrine but of spirit? If your brother speaks through the spirit, you will be washed and cleansed each time his spirit comes out and touches you, no matter how familiar the subject or how many times you have heard that particular theme. Any teaching or doctrine which does not result in reviving the spirit can only be considered as dead letter.

Again, there is something quite remarkable about one who is broken. If you are one who is indeed broken, you will find that you are not only able to give help but in the giving you also are helped. You are asked a question, and in answering it you are helped. You are praying with a sinner who is seeking the Lord, and again you are inwardly strengthened. You may be led to speak sternly with a brother who has slipped; not only is his spirit thereby revived but you too are inwardly built up. You are able to receive help from every spiritual contact. You marvel that the whole body is supplying you as a member. Any member of the body can supply your need, and you are helped. You become the recipient of the supply of the whole body. How rich it must be! You can truly rejoice: "The wealth of the Head is the body's, and the body's is mine." How greatly this differs from the mere increase of mental knowledge!

This ability to receive help—allowing another's spirit to touch our spirit—is proof that one is broken. Cleverness does not make it hard to be helped; rather, it is evidence that the outer shell is harder than others. In the Lord's mercy, a clever person must be drastically dealt with, broken many times and in many ways until one day he is able to receive the supply of the whole church. Let us ask ourselves, "Are we able to receive this supply from others?" If we cannot receive, it is likely that our hard shell hinders meeting the spirit of our brother when it is released. But if we are broken, as soon as his spirit moves, we are helped. The question, then, is not how powerful is the spirit but have the spirits touched each other? It is this touching of spirits which revives and builds one up. What a necessity then for the outward man to be broken. There can be no question but that this constitutes the basic requirement for our being helped and for helping others.

Fellowship in the Spirit

While there are many different kinds of fellowship, there is spiritual fellowship which is much more than the exchange of ideas and opinions. It is the interaction of spirits. This kind of fellowship is possible only after our outward man is shattered and our spirit is thus released to touch the spirit of others. In this sharing of spirit we experience the fellowship of the saints and understand what the Scriptures mean by "fellowship in the spirit." It truly is a fellowship in the spirit, and not an interflow of ideas. By this fellowship in the spirit we can pray with one accord. Because many pray through their mind, independent of their spirit, it is hard for them to find another with the same mind who can pray in accord with them.

Anyone who is born anew and has the indwelling Holy Spirit can have fellowship with us. This is possible because our spirit is open for fellowship, ready to receive, and be received by, our brother's spirit. And thus we can touch the body of Christ, for we are the body. Can we comprehend it when we say that our spirits are the body of Christ? Indeed, "deep calleth unto deep" (Ps. 42:7). The depth of your being is calling for a touch of my depth; and I am calling for a touch of the depth of the whole church. Here is the fellowship of the deeps, the calling and the answering of one another. This is the one thing most necessary if we are to be useful before the Lord and properly touch the spirit of the church.

A Meekness Beyond Imitation

When we suggest that we must be meek, we are not trying to persuade you to act meek. If you do, you will soon find that even this man-made meekness needs to be destroyed. We must learn once and for all that human striving to imitate meekness is futile. All must be of the Holy Spirit, for He alone knows our need and will arrange circumstances leading to the breaking of our outward man.

It is our responsibility to ask God for light that we may recognize the mighty hand of the Holy Spirit and willingly submit to it, acknowledging that whatever He does is right. Let us not be horses and mules without understanding. Rather, let us hand ourselves over to the Lord for Him to work in us. As you give yourself to the Lord you will discover that His work actually began five or ten years before, though it seemingly has not produced any fruit in you. Today a change has come. At last you can pray, "Lord, I was blind, not knowing how Thou wast leading me. Now I see that Thou dost desire to break me. For this I surrender myself to Thee." Then all that was unfruitful for five or ten years begins to bear fruit. We find the Lord skillfully moving in to destroy many things of whose existence we had not even been aware. This is His master work: to deprive us of pride, self-love and self-exaltation, that our spirit may be liberated and exercised unto usefulness.

Two Related Questions

Two questions arise here for us to consider. Since the breaking of the outward man is the work of the Holy Spirit in defying man's imitation, should we try to stop any fleshly action we recognize; or must we wait passively until greater light comes from the Holy Spirit, the Doer of the work?

Surely it is right and proper that we should put a stop to every fleshly activity, but we must see how this is vastly different from imitating the Spirit's work. To illustrate: Though I am proud, I must refuse all pride, yet I do not feign to be humble. Or, I can lose my temper with people, but I keep it under control; yet this does not make me gentle. So long as the negative is struggling for recognition, I should resist it without letup. Nevertheless, I should not pretend to possess the positive. This is the important distinction: pride is a negative thing, so I must deal with it; humility is something positive; therefore, I cannot imitate it. Though I must put a stop to all fleshly activities known to me, I do not need to imitate the positive virtue. All I need to do is to commit myself to the Lord, saying: "Lord, there is no reason to exert my strength to imitate. I am trusting Thee to do the work." External imitation is not of God; it is of man. All who seek the Lord must learn from within, not just conform outwardly. We must allow God to finish His work within us *before* we can expect the evidence of this to be manifest without. Whatever is manufactured externally is unreal and doomed to destruction. One who unwittingly possesses a counterfeit defrauds others as well as himself. As counterfeit behavior multiplies, the person himself comes to believe that such is his real self. Often it is hard to convince him of his unrealness, for he cannot distinguish the true from the false. Therefore, we must not try to imitate outwardly. It is far better to be natural; this opens the way for God to work in us. Let us be simple and not imitate anything, in the confidence that the Lord Himself will add His virtues to us.

The second question is: Some are naturally endowed with such a virtue as gentleness; is there a difference between natural gentleness and the gentleness that comes through discipline?

There are two points to be considered in answering this question. First, all that is natural is independent of the spirit, while all that comes through the discipline of the Holy Spirit is under the spirit's control, moving only as the spirit moves. Natural gentleness can really become a hindrance to the spirit. One who is habitually gentle is gentle in himself, not "in the Lord." Suppose the Lord wants him to stand up and utter some strong words. His natural gentleness will hinder him from following the Lord. He would say instead, "Ah, this I cannot do. I have never in my life uttered such hard words. Let someone else do it. I simply cannot." You see how his natural gentleness is not under the spirit's control. Anything that is natural has its own will and is independent of the spirit. However, that gentleness which comes through brokenness can be used by the spirit, for it does not resist nor offer its own opinion.

Second, a naturally gentle person is gentle only while you are going along with his will. If you force him to do what he does not like, he will change his attitude. In so-called human virtues, the element of self-denial is lacking. It is obvious that the purpose of all of them is to build up and establish our self-life. Whenever that self is violated, the human virtues all disappear. The virtues which spring from discipline, on the other hand, are only possessed after our ugly self-life has been destroyed. Where God is breaking your self, there true virtue is seen. The more self is wounded, the brighter shines true gentleness. Natural gentleness and spiritual fruit, then, are basically different.

A Final Exhortation

Having stressed the importance of the outward man being broken, let us be careful lest we try to effect this artificially. We must submit ourselves under the mighty hand of God, accepting all the necessary dealings. As the outward man is broken, the inward is strengthened. A few may find the inward man still feeble. Do not pray for strength to correct this, for the Bible commands us, "Be strong." Proclaim that it is your goal to be strong. The marvelous thing is that after your outward man is broken, you can be strong whenever you want to. The problem of strength is solved with the problem of the outward man. By desiring to be strong, you are strong. None can block your way. The Lord says, "Be strong." In the Lord you also say, "Be strong." And you find you are strong.

The inward man is freed only after the outward man is broken. This is the basic road to God's service.